HOW TO STOP FEELING GUILTY

DR VERNON COLEMAN worked as a GP in the Midlands for ten years, and is now a professional author and broadcaster. He was the UK's first TV 'agony uncle', and has written over thirty books explaining medicine to the lay reader, including *Stress and Your Stomach, Women's Problems – an A–Z, Overcoming Stress* and *Bodypower* for Sheldon Press. Dr Coleman is a Fellow of the Royal Society of Medicine and lives in a cottage on the North Devon coast. His magazine and newspaper columns are read regularly by millions of readers around the world, and his books have been translated into eleven languages and have sold well over a million copies.

Overcoming Common Problems

A successful and popular series to give you practical
help for the emotional and medical problems of
everyday life.

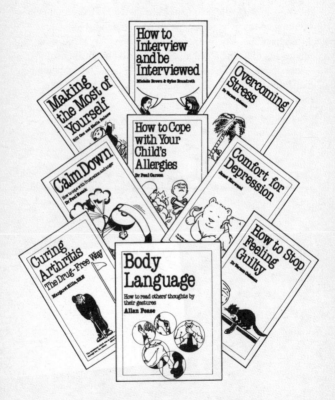

Paperbacks £1·95 to £4·95
Available from all good bookshops

 For a complete list of titles write to;
Sheldon Press Mail Order,
SPCK, Marylebone Road, London NW1 4DU

HOW TO STOP FEELING GUILTY

Dr Vernon Coleman

SHELDON PRESS
LONDON

First published in Great Britain in 1982 by
Sheldon Press, SPCK, Marylebone Road, London NW1 4DU
as *Guilt: Why it happens and how to overcome it*

Copyright © Vernon Coleman 1982

Third impression 1989

Typeset by Memo Typography Ltd
Nicosia, Cyprus
Printed and bound in Great Britain by
Biddles Ltd, Guildford and King's Lynn

ISBN 0 85969 549 2

Contents

AUTHOR'S NOTE

In all the case histories throughout this book I have changed the names of the individuals concerned. I have also made other changes where I consider they may be needed to protect the guilty.

VERNON COLEMAN
is an author
and general medical practitioner

1

A Universal Problem

Guilt is an emotion that is as common as love and as damaging as hate. Like love and hate it is something that affects most of us nearly all the time. Only fanatics and psychopaths remain entirely free of guilt for life.

Fanatics don't know what guilt is because they are so filled with a feeling of righteous indignation that there is no room for any self-doubt. Because they are driven by some force that seems greater and more powerful than anything else they never have to worry about other people. The single driving obsession that gives fire to the fanatic leaves no room for feelings such as regret and shame which are themselves the basic materials with which the rest of us make our guilt.

Psychopaths remain free of guilt because they are free of the sort of feelings that the rest of us describe as love and compassion—emotions which lead directly or indirectly to guilt. The psychopath cares nothing for others and little for himself. Without caring it is impossible to feel guilt.

The truth about guilt is that although a certain amount of it is caused by genuine evil-doing most guilty feelings are inspired not by any dreadful crime or great wrong-doing but by self-criticism and by feelings of inadequacy; the self-criticism and the feelings of inadequacy often having been inspired by our own inability to match the expectations held by ourselves and by those closest to us. Guilt is inextricably linked to love and compassion. Those who love the most and have the greatest feelings for the people around them are most likely to suffer from guilt.

Guilt is difficult to define precisely but in practical terms it is hard to distinguish it from what we commonly call our 'conscience'. Traditionally religious leaders have always taught that when we hear our conscience talking we're really listening to the voice of God. The priest will claim that the married man who has an affair with his secretary and suffers pangs of guilt or is troubled by his conscience is really being punished by God. The woman who neglects her mother and then feels bad about it suffers because God has been annoyed by her callousness.

The answer, says the priest, is to confess, to make your peace with God, to ask for His forgiveness and to live a purer life. But is that really the whole answer? When we feel guilty is it simply because God is spitefully making us suffer? It seems an odd and slightly roundabout way for an all powerful creator to act. Would God really behave in such a human way?

I don't think so, and I don't think that the traditional view of guilt is the right one. I believe that the feeling of guilt we suffer when we think we have done wrong is an entirely internal phenomenon. It is something that we do to ourselves because we feel that we have failed. We may have failed to do something we feel that we should have done. Or we may have done something that we feel we shouldn't have done. Either way the result is the same; we torture ourselves with self-recrimination. Having prosecuted ourselves we find ourselves guilty.

Whether we feel guilty because of what we have done, because of the effect it has had on others, or simply because we have been caught and exposed the results are very much the same. What we do to appease the feelings of self-criticism which accompany guilt varies according to the nature of the crime. When feelings of guilt are inspired by specific events for which we feel justifiably responsible it isn't too difficult to decide what we need to do in order to get rid of the guilt.

A woman who has stolen a packet of biscuits from a supermarket may get rid of the guilt she feels by sending an anonymous letter to the manager with a sum of money en-

2

closed. With that simple action she pays her debt and clears away her own guilt. A man who has damaged a neighbour's car when parking can call round and confess and offer to pay for the damage to be repaired. Again, by offering to right the wrong that has been done he hopes to eradicate his own feelings of guilt. In these cases, of course, the crime is small and easy to put right. The guilt is also easy to get rid of. Confession and paying penance are good for the soul.

It is no coincidence that in all major religions sinners are encouraged to do both. In some religions the priests even do their best to make confessions as painless as possible by isolating it from the crime. The Catholic penitent, for example, is allowed to make his peace directly with God, thereby avoiding the embarrassment of having to make reparation directly to the individual who has been offended or harmed.

Life would be very simple if all our guilts were as easy to get rid of. Unfortunately, it isn't always easy to define the cause of a feeling of guilt. And if you don't know why you feel guilty then it is difficult to do anything about it. If you don't even recognize that the suffering you're going through is produced by guilt then solving the problem is even more difficult.

What many of us perhaps fail to realize is just how widespread feelings of guilt are in our society. The amount of guilt that can be related directly to obvious offences such as shoplifting or damaging a neighbour's property make up just a minute proportion of the total. Guilt is one of the most powerful and most damaging human emotions. However strong and emotionally well-built we may consider ourselves to be there are very few of us who can honestly claim to have never suffered the agonies of guilt.

And there is something else too. Something which makes understanding and cradicating guilt even more difficult. Although guilt is an internal phenomenon, something we do to ourselves, it is very often produced by the

3

conscious or unconscious reactions of those around us. And invariably the people who do most to make us feel guilty are those who are closest to us. Guilt is a destructive force that is built on love and compassion. The more people we love and the greater our sense of compassion the greater the chances that we'll suffer from guilt.

Depression and nervous breakdown

Consider Mrs Linda Grosvenor. Until she married she worked as a secretary to the Managing Director of a middle-sized company. It was a demanding and rewarding job. She had a great deal of responsibility and earned a good salary. She worked for a year after she married and when she became pregnant she gave up her job.

When the youngest of her two children started school Mrs Grosvenor decided to resume her career. She had no qualms at all about taking what seemed to her to be a perfectly logical step. She wanted to live a useful and productive life in her own right. Her husband, proud of being an enlightened spouse happily encouraged her to find a job and took her out to celebrate when she eventually got a position with her old firm.

Everything went well for the first few months. Then there was a bit of a crisis at the office one day and Mrs Grosvenor was half-an-hour late getting home from work. She couldn't have left any earlier without letting her colleagues down badly. When she finally got home she found the children standing in the porch sheltering from the rain. The youngest was crying. No one said anything but being a sensitive mother Mrs Grosvenor felt bad about it.

During the following weeks and months there were a number of other, similar occasions. There was no one available to go to young Peter's sports day when he came second in the high jump. And because neither parent was available Sarah had to stay at home instead of going to a

4

riend's birthday party. Slowly problems came to the surface a little more openly.

'Mummy', said Peter one evening, 'my teacher was going to ring you up today because I had a headache; but I told her that you'd be at work.'

'Darling,' said her husband, one evening as they sat watching the late film together, 'if you have time could you make some of those buns you always used to make? We've not had any of those for ages.'

Those gentle comments were never intended to produce any feelings of guilt. But they did. Slowly Mrs Grosvenor began to suffer more and more as she was torn between her commitment to her family, her commitment to her colleagues at work and her commitment to herself and her own ambitions.

When I saw her she was depressed, unable to sleep, not eating properly and desperately unhappy. It was impossible to treat these symptoms until the underlying sense of guilt had been dealt with and she had learnt to come to terms with what she could and could not justifiably expect of herself.

Slowly, insidiously, her family and her colleagues, the people who were closest to her and who meant the most to her, had produced an enormous burden of guilt which Mrs Grosvenor was unable to cope with. She had gradually begun to feel inadequate and aware that she wasn't satisfying the expectations of those who were closest to her. Her children weren't getting the sort of attention that other children seemed to be getting. And her husband had gently made it clear that he considered himself deprived. The greater the love the greater the guilt.

For Mrs Grosvenor there was no quick, simple, easy solution. She couldn't solve her problem with a single confession, letter of apology or sum of money. She couldn't serve a jail sentence and be released entirely free of guilt. She had to learn to live with her problems and with the expectations of those around her. Guilt cannot always be banished because often there is no simple solution which will satisfy everyone.

Agonies like this are common and they affect us all. The out-of-work father whose son wants a new bike for Christmas will feel guilty if he cannot provide one. He'll feel that he has failed his son. The married woman who is still treated as a young girl by her own mother will feel guilty if she doesn't accept her mother's advice when choosing curtains. At the same time she will feel guilty because she knows that she is allowing her mother to interfere with the running of her own home. She will feel that she has failed herself and her husband.

Then there are the guilts which we feel when we sense that we have failed to honour the principles which we have been taught to consider as inviolable. Most of us have, for example, been brought up to consider work a daily responsibility. We feel guilty if we aren't working and we may find relatation difficult to enjoy. It is this need to work, and the accompanying sense of guilt which we suffer when we don't work, which makes so many people spend their weekends carefully cleaning the car or weeding the garden. We may not want to clean the car, we may not enjoy weeding the garden, but feel guilty if we aren't doing something. In addition we will feel guilty if we allow the car to stay dirty or the garden to stay scruffy because then neighbours and passers-by will be able to see obvious signs of our failure to work. We end up doing work we don't want to do and don't need to do simply because we've been led to believe that we have a duty and a responsibility to work.

Guilt is a driving force which most of us find irresistible. And in the end it can often have disastrous effects. I know that many of the patients I see who are suffering from anxiety and depression are ill because they have been slowly tortured and bewildered by guilt. Confused and uncertain they eventually begin to show signs of developing what is commonly called a nervous breakdown.

George Taylor had been a sales representative for the whole of his adult life. He had started on the road at the age of 19, working for a manufacturer of children's toys, and moved at the age of 25 to a firm making sweets. He is a gentle, kind man with an extremely easy-going manner. I suspect that everyone he meets finds him easy to talk to and likeable.

At the age of 40 Mr Taylor was offered a post as an area sales manager. The promotion inevitably carried with it a higher salary, a better car and a number of other minor perks. Mr Taylor tried it for a month but after a life of travelling just couldn't get used to the idea of working in an office all the time. He asked for his old job back. Reluctantly the bosses at the company's head office agreed. I think they'd already suspected that Mr Taylor wasn't going to be as successful as a sales manager as he'd been as a sales representative.

Although he was happier once he was on the road again Mr Taylor's problems were only just beginning. The major problem was that his wife had been rather taken with the idea of being married to a sales manager instead of a sales representative. She'd enjoyed the extra status and the larger car and for the first time in her life she'd enjoyed having her husband with her every evening. So Mr Taylor began to feel guilty. He felt that he'd let his wife down and that by turning down the chance of a better job and more money he'd failed her in a very important way.

When he first came to me for help he was already exhibiting many of the classical signs of a nervous breakdown. He was getting irritable and forgetting appointments for the first time in his life. He was no longer able to get through as much work as he'd always been able to manage quite successfully and he began to lose his flair for getting on with people. In addition he started having accidents in the car. In fact I first saw him when he came along to the surgery to

7

have some stitches removed from a cut in his forehead.

Before I could help Mr Taylor I had to help him understand exactly what was at the root of his problem. Only by coming to terms with his feelings of inadequacy and guilt could he hope to deal effectively with his more immediate symptoms.

Ulcers and anger

Of course, many people don't just show mental signs of stress and strain. Guilt can also produce real physical damage. Stomach ulcers, asthma, eczema and heart disease are just four of the common physical disorders which are well known to be caused directly by anxiety and worry and indirectly, therefore, by guilt.

Miss Rachel Phelps, for example, came to see me complaining of pains in her stomach. An examination and an X-ray quickly showed that she had a duodenal ulcer. Talking to Miss Phelps, an attractive, slender, 41-year-old, I found that she had lived with her mother all her life. Her mother, a sufferer from heart disease and arthritis, needed almost continuous nursing care and Miss Phelps had dedicated herself to providing that nursing care.

Then when she'd perhaps abandoned all ideas of romance Miss Phelps had unexpectedly met a widower and started going out with him. It was the first time since she'd been a teenager that she ever had any sort of relationship with a man. Ironically, she'd first met him while accompanying her mother on a routine visit to the hospital out patient department. Her new lover had been visiting an elderly aunt dying of cancer and love had blossomed over the coffee vending machine in the hospital corridor.

The relationship had begun as a purely platonic one but after the affair had been going on for two months it secretly moved on to a more physical level. Miss Phelps found to her surprise that this new relationship was pleasing and

8

satisfying in many different ways. But it was a bitter-sweet discovery for at the same time she began to feel an overwhelming sense of guilt.

First, because she sensed that her mother would disapprove of her having, let alone enjoying, any sort of sexual relationship. And second because she knew that she could never put her relationship on a permanent footing without allowing her mother to be placed in some sort of residential home. To do that would make her feel that she had failed her mother. Not to do it made her feel that she had failed both her lover and herself. And so a previously healthy woman, who had never even experienced so much as a twinge of indigestion, developed a painful and very real ulcer in her duodenum.

Guilt can also have more subtle effects on our lives. It can encourage us to distort the truth, to deceive ourselves and to become unusually aggressive in our attempts to defend ourselves from ourselves. We may try to avoid the consequence of our own guilt by seeking to put the blame for our own omissions and commissions onto others.

While I was on emergency duty last weekend, for example, there was an occasion when a patient turned his own feelings of guilt into aggression which he directed at me. On Saturday evening at about eleven I had a telephone call from Mr Yarborough. The Yarboroughs have been patients of mine for several years and there has never been any friction between us before, but when I spoke to Mr Yarborough on the telephone he seemed unreasonably angry.

The problem concerned their young son, Philip, who is nearly nine. When I got there, some twenty minutes after the telephone call, I found that as his father had reported he was crying with the pain of an inflamed and infected ear. Even as I wrote out the necessary prescription and rummaged in my bag for a small packet of the appropriate antibiotic so that treatment could be started right away Mr

9

Yarborough began to shout abuse at me. He wanted to know why I'd failed to prevent his son developing an ear infection and why I'd taken so long to turn out. Sprinkling his verbal onslaught with a good selection of adjectives he threatened to report me to the nearest Police Station, blacken my eye and ruin me financially.

With some difficulty I managed to persuade him to sit down and talk to me. I found out that at seven that evening he and his wife had left their young son in the care of a fifteen-year-old babysitter. Before they'd left young Philip had begun to cry and complain of a pain in his ear but Mr and Mrs Yarborough, anxious not to be late for the film they wanted to see, had fed him an aspirin tablet and told him to be quiet. When they returned and found Philip in pain and the babysitter distraught they'd been overtaken with guilt. That guilt has been quickly turned into aggression and the only outsider available as a target for the aggression had been their general practitioner.

There is no doubt that guilt affects nearly all of us in one way or another. But whatever way it has its effects, whether as long standing anxiety or as an apparently straight-forward physical disorder, guilt is debilitating, pointless and painful.

It is possible to argue that if we never felt guilty we would all be behaving with the callous disregard for others that fanatics and psychopaths exhibit, but the long, cruel, lingering pangs which most of us suffer as a result of the guilt we feel are too often out of all proportion. There are no slick and simple answers to the problems posed by feelings of guilt and we can never abolish guilt from our minds entirely, but there is much that we can do to deal effectively with its consequences and improve our capacity to cope with it.

2

The Sources of Guilt

It is impossible to classify all the different ways in which guilt develops. But for the sake of simplicity I have divided the various sources of guilt into two main groups. Those which stem from personal relationships and those related to our role in society.

Within personal relationships guilt is produced subtly and even unintentionally. This can happen when, for example, one partner says to another heading off out for the evening, 'Don't worry about me, I'll be all right'. Those few simple words, apparently and perhaps deliberately intended to eradicate any feelings of guilt are, in fact, just as likely to arouse guilt.

Sometimes guilt is introduced far more crudely and far more deliberately. As, for example, when a father says to a disobedient son, 'Your mother has had a nervous breakdown worrying about you'. That sort of emotional blackmail is deliberately designed to induce a sense of guilt in the son. It may be that there is no other way to capture any sympathy or understanding from the son.

By and large the ease with which we develop feelings of guilt depends on the closeness of the relationship concerned. Our expectations, hopes and fears are greatest when relationships are close and we tend to feel guilt more readily when we feel that we may have failed someone close to us. Consequently it is in our dealings with immediate members of our families, close friends and lovers that much guilt originates.

The second type of guilt is a result of society's teachings, expectations and demands. Most of us have an inbuilt concept of right and wrong and if we trespass according to that inbuilt concept then we feel guilty.

11

What we often forget is that those feelings are not so much inherited as learned. They are simply social prejudices which have been established by instruction and example. Most of us feel guilty if we steal because it is considered anti-social in most civilized communities. Other feelings of guilt develop from prejudices which are more difficult to understand. We feel guilty if we show our affection in public, if we enjoy ourselves, if we lie in bed on a Sunday morning or if we earn too much money, but it isn't always easy to understand exactly why we feel guilty in those circumstances.

When we try to find out why guilt develops we find that there are a number of different potential sources. Very many of our feelings of guilt are inspired by behavioural patterns to which we were exposed when young. Schoolteachers, for example, will commonly claim that if they are given charge of young children they can mould the minds of those children completely. Nevertheless, despite the undisputed power of teachers of all kinds, religion is probably an even greater guilt producer. Religious leaders have for centuries recognized and taken advantage of the fact that feelings of guilt can be used to subdue self-confidence and assertiveness and to produce an obedient, malleable congregation.

In addition to teachers and priests there are today very many modern guilt-building forces. For example, as a result of the ideas put forward by those who support the equality of women in the fullest economic, social and political sense, many men and women feel guilty whatever attitude they adopt towards one another. Men feel guilty if they treat women as equals because that conflicts with what they were taught as children. But they also feel guilty if they treat women as nothing more than delicate, vulnerable, feminine creatures in need of support.

Women suffer just as much from this conflict between guilt-building prejudices. They have to satisfy their well established desires to look after husband, children and home. But at the same time they have to satisfy their desires to establish their own identities as people rather than wives and mothers. The conflicts between these guilt-building forces mean that a great deal of additional guilt is produced.

Obviously, the types of guilt which result from personal relationships and from social prejudices combine and inter-link in very many ways. Generally speaking, whereas it is our personal relationships which usually produce specific instances of guilt, it is the guilt-builders who make us susceptible to guilt and who make some individuals far more vulnerable to guilt than others.

3

Personal Relationships

There is no relationship closer than that between child and parent. And there is no relationship more likely to produce deep-seated feelings of guilt.

I suppose that when most of us think of guilt-ridden children we think of the typical fictional Jewish mother who has dedicated her life to caring for her son. Apparently concerned with nothing other than her son's happiness she will make it clear to everybody around, with a great show of self sacrifice, that she has dedicated her life to protecting him from the evils of the world.

No one is more skilled than she in using guilt as a weapon with which to manipulate her unfortunate offspring. I still remember with a shiver of fear the mother of a friend of mine at medical school. He wasn't Jewish and neither was she but I've never met anyone who fitted more precisely the classical pattern of the awe-inspiring Jewish mother.

A week after Terry had left home for the first time his mother arrived on the doorstep of our flat accompanied by the family doctor and an armful of drugs. She was, she said, convinced that he must be ill since she hadn't heard a word from him. Distraught with worry she'd come prepared to find her only son pale and trembling on his death bed. Naturally the heavy hint was taken and for the rest of his time at medical school Terry rang home every two days.

When he got involved with a girlfriend his mother quickly made it clear that she wasn't prepared to relinquish any of her maternal authority. Indeed, with a few well chosen words she succeeded in recruiting her potential daughter-in-law as a sort of on-the-spot representative.

'Terry has always been a wonderful son to me,' she explained 'and because he's all I've got it means so much to

14

me to know that he's being well looked after.'

Even when they married the maternal ties weren't broken. Indeed, if anything, the knot was tied even tighter when the first grandchild came along. With comments like, 'The baby must have grown a lot by now perhaps you could send me a photograph of him?' and 'you'll soon discover that having children isn't all sunshine and roses. You wait until he's grown up and doesn't have time for you', she succeeded in keeping the feelings of guilt in top condition.

When he had been appointed a consultant surgeon and had acquired all the trappings of social and economic success Terry still found it impossible to eradicate those maternal influences. If he didn't ring home every couple of days he was wracked with guilt. If he didn't consult his mother when he planned to change his car or buy a new suit or make some arrangements concerning the children he felt overwhelmed with shame. And when, once or twice, he tried to break free he soon found that his mother was more than ready for him.

Once, after he'd failed to call for a week he received a frantic telephone call from a neighbour telling him that his mother had collapsed. When he tried to ring there was no reply. So he had no alternative but to drive 180 miles to find her sitting up in bed munching chocolates and sipping sherry. In his relief at discovering that she hadn't died of a broken heart he didn't even remember to remonstrate with her.

On another occasion when he decided not to invite her to stay for Christmas she wrote and told him how a local charity group had kindly taken her a luncheon and a small Christmas parcel. It wasn't quite the same as having a family Christmas, she said, but it was kind of strangers to give up part of their Christmas to help ease the loneliness of an old lady.

Not all parents are that manipulative, of course. But even the most thoughtful and undemanding parents can unconsciously produce enormous pressures. In the end all children are subjected to some pressures from their parents.

The greater the love, the greater the guilt

Paradoxically the more loving and devoted parents are the greater the guilt will be. Sigmund Freud would argue that all boys feel guilt towards their fathers because of their unconscious sexual desires for their mothers, while girls feel guilty towards their mothers because of their equally unconscious sexual desires for their fathers. But we needn't even attempt to assess the value of these arguments in order to see exactly how guilt can arise during what may well appear to be a perfect parent-child relationship.

The fact is that the more loving parents are, and the more they do for their children the greater the impossibility of those children ever being able to repay all the love and devotion that has been shown. The child whose parents have made sacrifices for him or her will be aware of those sacrifices without any conscious reference being made to them. As the child matures and gradually becomes aware of all that has been done on his behalf he will slowly realize that there is no way that he can ever repay all that kindness. He will forever be in debt if his parents have been kind and supportive. And the kinder and more generous they have been the greater the debt will be.

Any debt that cannot be paid in full, particularly an emotional one, will lead to a feeling of guilt, a feeling that can easily be enhanced in any one of a thousand small ways. It is common enough to hear parents say things like, 'We want you to have the chances that we didn't have'. This can only make it that much clearer to the child that he or she does indeed have kind or thoughtful parents who are prepared to make sacrifices on his or her behalf. And even the most careful and thoughtful parents can easily find themselves making statements like 'If you loved me you

16

wouldn't do that' when all other disciplinary moves seem to have failed temporarily.

The unconscious principle there is that if you can't get children to do things you want them to do because they love you then you make it clear that as far as you're concerned if they don't do what you want them to do then they don't love you. And you leave them struggling to cope with the guilt that this psychological stranglehold induces.

On the surface making children feel guilty may appear far less cruel than shouting, screaming or even offering physical punishment. After all the man who hits his children with a leather belt is pretty obviously hurting them and causing direct pain. Nevertheless, the fact is that inducing guilt is a very damaging way to punish children. Parents who do not physically punish their children and who don't even shout at them can cause real emotional havoc by simply making it clear that they have been hurt and disappointed. A quick physical punishment is soon forgotten and fairly easily dismissed. But the parents who show that they are hurt can produce long-lasting feelings of guilt among their children.

I remember looking after one family in which both parents proudly claimed never to have punished their children at all. And while it is true that they didn't hit them, send them to bed without any supper or stop their pocket money they punished them far more cruelly than any other parents I've ever known.

The father, a headmaster, would take the errant child on one side and carefully explain just how hurt he was by whatever it was that the child had done wrong. He would point out that he had been unable to sleep or eat properly and that he was so full of shame that he had been unable to hold his head up at work. This would go on for days at a time and each episode would merge into the next. The result was that the children were dominated by their feelings of guilt, worthlessness and shame. Both children needed psychiatric care before they reached the age of 16.

Another mother I knew would repeatedly tell her son that 'Young Ronnie is so good to his mother. I only hope she appreciates just how lucky she is.' Only the most callous and unloving child could fail to feel a pang of guilt for not being as good and as loving as young Ronnie.

Re-assessing our parents

As children we do not, of course, have much control over the extent of the guilt we acquire from our parents. But as we mature we can look at our relationships with our parents and try to see just how much guilt is involved in the way we feel towards them. It is probably impossible to eradicate all the hoarded guilt which can be built by deliberately manipulative parents but it is nevertheless possible to become aware of the existence of guilt as an influence.

We should try to be honest with ourselves and to assess as accurately as possible the nature of our relationships with our parents.

Do we do things because we love our parents or because we feel guilty if we don't? And just how much of the guilt we feel is a result of our having been manipulated?

Meanwhile, as we ourselves become parents we can at least be aware of the ways in which parents can, consciously and unconsciously, produce feelings of guilt in their children.

Parents feel guilty too

Parents don't only produce guilt in their children they are also potential sufferers themselves.

It is quite common today for young mothers to have jobs and responsibilities outside the home. Some mothers work simply because they get bored if they don't; others work to help increase the size of the family income. Whatever the reason for a woman working the chances are that at some stage or another in her career she will begin to suffer pangs of guilt.

Mrs Wilson, for example, worked as a physiotherapist in a local hospital and found her job immensely satisfying. The pleasure she got from her job did not, however, prevent her from feeling guilty about the fact that her two children, aged 10 and 12, had to stay at school for dinner, had to make their own way to school and back home in the evening and had to let themselves into the house on the evenings when she didn't beat them home. She came to see me for advice because she'd become quite seriously depressed. She was torn between her need to have a life outside the home and her natural maternal desire to provide her children with a comfortable, complete and happy home life.

'The trouble is,' she told me, 'that about a year ago before I started working I was going insane with the drudgery of just looking after the house. I remember one day when I spent two-and-a-half hours looking for a missing sock. I was elated when I found it but when I suddenly realized just what had happened to my life I was suicidal for nearly a week. Life just didn't seem worth living.' She confessed that she began to resent her children for tying her to the house. Then she began to feel guilty for resenting them.

'On the days when I didn't feel guilty for wanting to go out to work', she told me, 'I felt guilty because I didn't feel guilty. Somehow I felt I was wrong to want a life outside the home; to want to do something for myself.'

Once she started working she began to feel much brighter. 'I felt that I became a much more interesting person,' she said. 'I was more relaxed and I honestly think I got on better with the children. Before I went to work I'd become rather obsessional. You know, I was one of those mums who never seem to stop nagging. Once I'd got a job that I enjoyed I seemed more able to put up with the fact that the children seemed determined to leave their bedrooms festooned with dirty laundry and bits of paper.'

It was only when she'd been at work for some months that Mrs Wilson began to feel that she was perhaps letting her children down.

'No one actually complained.' she said. 'It was just that I felt bad about things. Perhaps because I felt so much happier now than I did before.'

I asked her whether she thought the children were happier now than they had been before.

'Its difficult to answer that.' she said. 'But I definitely think that I get on better with them now than I did before.'

That seemed to be a most significant comment. I pointed out to Mrs Wilson that life must inevitably consist of a sequence of compromises. She had to make up her mind whether the disadvantages of her working were greater or less than the disadvantages of her not working.

'If you are happier and your family is happier when you're working,' I explained, 'then surely the problems that are produced are worth learning to cope with?'

I tried to explain to her that mothers who work and who enjoy their jobs are often better mothers than they would be if they didn't have responsibilities outside the house.

Divided loyalties

Of course it isn't only mothers who suffer from guilt as a result of their relationships with their children. Fathers suffer too.

An increasing number of men in early middle age are today beginning to ask themselves exactly what they're getting out of life. I remember one particular patient of mine, Mr George Norman, explaining to me exactly how he felt as he approached his fortieth birthday.

'I feel as though I've lost my own identity altogether,' he

confessed. 'Sometimes I think that my only function in life is to pay an unending series of bills and to be available with money to pay for all the necessary and unnecessary things that three teenage children demand'. It was, he said, rather like struggling to cope with the insatiable demands of three baby cuckoos.

'When I was younger I wanted to be a musician,' he explained, 'but I earned more money from my job as a quality control supervisor in a local car component factory. I played the double bass in a little dance band but gradually I gave it up. We didn't make much money and I found I could earn more working overtime at the factory. Now I feel that I've missed out on life. I feel resentful. And I feel guilty because I feel resentful. Half of me tells me that I have a responsibility to provide for my family. Half of me tells me that I have a responsibility to myself.'

Mr Norman was so torn by his divided loyalties and his guilty feelings that when I saw him he wasn't sleeping properly, wasn't eating and had even begun to toy with the idea of just disappearing.

'I have these day-dreams of just catching a train somewhere or driving to the airport and just going abroad.' he told me.

I asked him if he'd talked to his wife and children and discussed his feelings. He confessed that he hadn't.

'Don't you think it might help?' I asked. I pointed out that if he didn't discuss his anxieties and resentments with his family then he couldn't hope to get rid of them.

'You'll just continue to store up these feelings and feel guiltier and guiltier both about having such feelings and about having failed to do the things you'd like to do.' I told him. 'There isn't a simple answer, but perhaps you can join a dance band again. Perhaps the family can cut down their demands a little. Perhaps the teenagers could get part-time jobs of their own to help pay their way.'

'I'd probably feel bad about failing to look after the

family properly,' moaned Mr Norman.

'That's something you've got to face.' I insisted. 'You can't eradicate all sources of guilt. You can only try and come to terms with your guilt.'

I tried to convince him that he wasn't alone in his feelings and that such agonies are common. When I saw him recently he told me that he'd joined a small dance band again. No one in the family seemed to be suffering. Everyone was much happier.

Sex: the hot bed of guilt

Although I certainly wouldn't support Freud who argued that just about all human relationships depend in one way or another on sex I do believe that sex is one of the most important driving forces and influences on the way we behave. And because sexual instincts, demands and expectations are so important there are very many ways in which our sexual relationships with others can lead to the development of feelings of guilt.

Here is an almost classical case of a young girl and her boyfriend. Julie Carter was just 16 when she started to date a boy two years older than herself. She met him at a school discotheque. After a couple of evening visits to the cinema they found themselves babysitting for Julie's older sister. And it was in her sister's front room that Julie was exposed to one of the oldest blackmail tricks known to man or woman. When she tried to halt her boyfriend's advances he insisted that if she loved him she'd let him make love to her.

She successfully resisted that trick but found his threat to leave her and find another girlfriend more difficult to deal with. When he complained that she'd led him on and that he would probably be physically damaged if she continued to refuse to let him make love to her she could no longer cope with the accumulated guilt.

She felt guilty because she feared that there might be

something in what he said. After all she hadn't resisted when he had simply wanted to kiss her. And together with the guilt she felt a mixture of other emotions. She was desperately in love with him. She was frightened that he would leave her if she didn't do what he wanted. She was also afraid that if she held out too long he would be justified in believing that she didn't love him.

And so she gave in.

That was when her problems really started. Even before she'd got home she was beginning to suffer real pangs of guilt. Her main fear was that if her mother and father found out they would be ashamed of her. She wasn't frightened of them being cross as much as of their being hurt. When she missed her next period and realized that she was pregnant the guilt really began to pile up. And by the time she'd had an abortion she felt as full of guilt as if she'd been a mass murderer for the whole of her life. All that guilt began with her simply attempting to avoid hurting her boyfriend's feelings. One small potential guilt led to a veritable guilt landslide.

Events are not always as dramatic or as straightforward as that. I well remember treating one young woman who had an apparently wholesome relationship with her steady boyfriend but who came to ask for help when she found herself worrying about the fact that she was enjoying sex. She'd been brought up in a house where sexual matters were considered dirty and where sex was considered something rather improper. Her mother had led her to believe that only whores and nymphomaniacs actually enjoyed sex while all healthy, normal women endured it for the sake of their husbands.

When my patient found that she actively enjoyed intercourse and that she obtained great physical pleasure from her relationship she began to suffer enormous pangs of guilt. She felt that there had to be something wrong with her if she actually enjoyed sex. And it was with a tremendous sense of shame that she admitted that she frequently made the advances to her lover rather than the other way round.

The wider discussions of sexual matters which take place today in magazines, newspapers and books has led to another set of problems too. Many individuals whose sex drives are limited and whose own interest in sex is relatively slight actually feel guilty because of their apparent failure to enjoy and share a full sexual life.

Men, for example, who are aware of the elusive nature of the female orgasm and whose partners are aware of the glories of the multiple orgasm may find themselves feeling guilty if their performances fail to come up to a satisfactory standard. Impotence is such a common problem that there can be few males who have never failed to get it up on occasion. There are many simple reasons for a failure to obtain an erection. Simple tiredness being probably the commonest cause. And yet despite this men who fail to obtain an erection will undoubtedly feel guilty. They'll feel that they have failed in a most fundamental way.

The man's partner is equally likely to suffer from guilt. She'll feel that she has in some way let her man down. She'll feel guilty on her account and she maywell also feel guilty for having helped make him feel guilty. The ramifications are endless. It is hardly surprising that many single incidents of impotence lead to prolonged sexual problems.

The increase in the availability of sex manuals and the wide publicity given to the very many variations on the basic missionary position have led to many people feeling guilty about their sexual tastes. I've met men who have been full of guilt for having experimented with and enjoyed oral sex and I've met men who have been full of guilt for not having practised oral sex. And I've met as many men and women consumed with guilt for not having had and enjoyed countless explosive sexual encounters as I have men and women feeling guilty for having enjoyed sex too much.

An increasing number of men and women worry that their physical equipment is unsatisfactory. Men, for example, often seem to feel guilty about the size, thickness, length, circumference, shape, colour and breadth of their penises. It is today fairly common for young men to walk into the surgery and confess that they feel inadequate on such grounds. This is a type of guilt. What they are really saying is that they feel frightened that they won't be able to satisfy their women properly.

Women suffer similar fears. The thriving business in plastic surgery is ample proof of the fact that there are many hundreds of thousands of women who worry that their breasts are too big or too small; that their vaginas are too tight or too lax; that their nipples are too noticeable or too tiny. Again these are just variations on the guilt theme. The women are frightened that they will fail to satisfy their men according to the high standard set by society today. They feel guilty that they have failed to provide their men with the perfectly formed female body.

So although the truth is that shape and size of female or male sexual equipment is entirely irrelevant as far as satisfaction is concerned, millions of men and women continually feel guilty about what they consider to be the unsatisfactory state of their own bodies.

There are also the very different guilts which torment homosexuals. For example, one female patient of mine who admitted to being a lesbian and having a girl lover felt guilty not because of her relationship or because of anything she'd done in a physical sense but because she suspected that her parents and brothers strongly disapproved of her relationship.

And a male homosexual who had never married and who lived openly as a homosexual and campaigner for the Gay Lib movement admitted that deep down he still felt guilty because his lover had left his wife and family for him.

We all have an endless capacity for feeling guilty and sex

is an activity which offers more opportunities than most for the development of this guilt. It is, above all, an area of human behaviour which is very much under the influence of society's guilt-builders.

Friendship isn't all plain sailing

Many of the guilty feelings which arise between friends do so because of uncertainties about exactly what can and cannot be expected of a friendship. There are people who expect too much of their friends and eventually push them too far. That sort of behaviour can produce enormously damaging feelings of guilt. Consider Mrs Ruby Yallop.

Mrs Yallop had a job working in a large department store where she was responsible for buying children's clothes. She also had three young children of her own, all of them under the age of eight. Her neighbour, Mrs Enid Lawson, also had three young children but she didn't have a job.

Problems arose during the summer holidays when Mrs Yallop didn't quite know what to do with her children. The store didn't have a crêche and there were no suitable baby minders or nursery schools in the area. So, as the school holidays approached, Mrs Yallop asked her neighbour if she would be prepared to look after the children for her once or twice.

Mrs Lawson, being a generous woman and a kind neighbour, agreed without a moment's hesitation. Unfortunately, partly because she was too busy to make any other arrangements and partly because she just didn't know anyone else capable and prepared to help, Mrs Yallop ended up leaving her children with Mrs Lawson every day for the first fortnight of the school holidays.

That wasn't quite what Mrs Lawson had expected and it wasn't quite what she'd been prepared for. She'd looked forward to spending some time with her own children during the summer holidays. Running a nursery for six youngsters hadn't been her plan at all. So, after two weeks, Mrs Lawson popped a note through her neighbour's door one Sunday afternoon to let her know that she wouldn't be able to look after the young Yallops that week. She explained that she had to take her own children to visit relatives.

Mrs Yallop was furious. She didn't have any other friends to look after the children. And so she had to take a week off work. She made it clear that she thought Mrs Lawson had let her down badly. The previously good relationship between the two neighbours no longer existed.

Ironically it was Mrs Lawson who suffered the worst feelings of guilt. She felt bad because she had let her friend down. And she felt guilty because her note hadn't been entirely honest—she didn't have to visit relatives every day of the week. Mrs Yallop, who simply felt angry, bitter and disappointed didn't stop to think about whether or not she'd expected too much of her friend.

Simple social relationships can also lead to the development of many feelings of guilt. For example, dinner invitations that aren't returned often lead to mild guilt feelings. 'We must have the Smiths over for a meal,' says Mrs Jones, struggling to cope with recurring pangs of guilt.

At Christmas, there seem to be an endless number of ways in which friendship can lead to guilt. Someone who received an unexpected card will rush out and buy a card to return because otherwise they'll feel guilty about failing to reciprocate. Even presents which seem unequal can produce enormous feelings of guilt. If one girl buys another a couple of handkerchiefs for Christmas and receives in return an expensive bottle of perfume she'll feel dreadfully guilty. It's even possible that the friend who bought the perfume will herself feel guilty for having put her colleague in such a position.

In general, guilt is more likely to occur when for one reason or another one friend under or over estimates the value and extent of the friendship. When that happens, and the expectations of one person exceed the enthusiasms of the other, there are a great many ways in which guilt can ensue. And as it is with all other relationships the guilt is worse when the friendship is a close one. We quickly feel guilty when we have in some way offended or let down a close friend whereas if the friendship is slight and of little real significance we're much more likely to dismiss any problem that might arise.

Business relationships and
guilt that isn't quite so accidental

I doubt if even the most unscrupulous individuals would contemplate deliberately and cold-bloodedly making their friends feel guilty. There are, however, many instances in which people do use guilt quite deliberately. Predictably, perhaps, this happens most frequently where money is at stake.

Like all doctors in general practice I am often visited by drug company representatives. These men and women travel the country calling on doctors and hoping to be given the opportunity to describe the values and virtues of their company's latest drugs. One representative I know is a master at the art of manipulating the doctors he meets and making them feel guilty if they don't prescribe the products he promotes.

He'll begin each meeting with a doctor by talking about almost anything other than medicine or drugs. The only certain factor is that whatever he chooses as the subject for his conversation will be something of interest to the doctor concerned. He'll find out in advance what sort of things are likely to attract the doctor's keenest attention. A few words with the doctor's secretary or receptionist will usually be enough to unearth an interest in cricket, fishing, stamp-collecting or whatever. Then, during the conversation about cricket or stamp collecting, he'll find something that the doctor is really keen to acquire or to discover.

He might find out that Doctor Agnew has been trying to get tickets for a particular cricket match. Or he might discover that Doctor Young has been hunting for a particular rare book. That is always his cue to offer to help. And make no mistake about it he knows just how to offer exactly the right sort of help!

He always knows how to get hold of special match tickets, where to find rare books or stamps and where the best fish can be caught. He doesn't offer to provide any of these items. But he will offer to do the donkey work. He will never spend money on any of the doctors he meets. That would be crude and unforgivable. But he will offer to get hold of the required tickets or trace the rare stamp to a dealer, on his journeys round the country it isn't difficult to pop into a shop here or an office there.

Then, when he's made his offer, he will with carefully rehearsed reluctance, bring up the subject of his company's product. 'Have you managed to prescribe any of our Angipax?' he'll ask diffidently. And, of course, the doctor, anxious to repay his debt to his new friend will be keen to show interest in the product. If he wasn't already prescribing the drug concerned then he will certainly promise to do so.

Experienced shop assistants also use guilt to improve business. The shoe salesman, who is anxious to make a sale will happily fetch shoe after shoe and will eagerly run up and down his step ladder to fetch new boxes. Nothing will be too much trouble as he slowly makes the customer feel that a refusal would be positively ungrateful. It doesn't always work, of course, for some customers have a high threshold for such tricks. But it works often enough to make it worthwhile.

Similarly the car salesman will be eager to do everything for his potential customers. He'll open the car door for them. He'll run back to the office to fetch a brochure. He'll take them for a long drive. He'll flatter them. And he'll tell them that the price he's offering is so low that he'll probably get into trouble with his boss. The unsubtle will even claim that if they don't make a sale they'll lose their jobs.

All these tricks are used to ensure that the customer will eventually feel guilty if he doesn't buy the item on sale. He'll feel that he has let down the salesman by refusing to part with his money. Buying the shoes or the car or whatever is easier than coping with the guilt for many of us. That's why we so often find ourselves buying items we don't really want.

4

Social Pressures

Concentrate for a moment and try to think of the sort of thing you feel guilty about. The chances are that your list will contain the same thoughts and actions as the lists your neighbours, friends and relatives would compile.

When I asked Mr Timpson, a 43-year-old company director, to answer this question he at first simply told me that he felt guilty about not going to church and about not spending enough time with his children. Those two thoughts seemed to satisfy him for a moment but when I left him to think for a little longer he came up with a whole range of guilty thoughts. The list seemed to surprise him rather more than it surprised me.

He told me that he felt guilty about the fact that on a trip to Hamburg he'd visited a strip club. He felt guilty about buying and reading 'girlie' magazines and he felt guilty about the fact that he'd once been caught masturbating by a maiden aunt. He felt guilty about having 'borrowed' another boy's eraser at school and about having lied to his mother when he'd got home late after his first date.

Once the flow of memories had started it became difficult to stop them. He confessed that he felt guilty about the times he'd hidden behind the bicycle sheds to smoke cigarettes he'd taken from his father's cigarette case; that he'd felt guilty about not reading more of the classics by authors such as Dickens and Hardy and guilty about watching so much junk television. With a wry smile he agreed that he had been repressing many of these guilty feelings for years.

He explained that he also felt guilty about expecting his wife to stay at home, look after the house and the children and to provide him with meals and clean laundry. On the other hand he also felt guilty about the fact that he had recently insisted that his secretary came in to work even when her husband was sick in bed with influenza.

He confessed to feeling guilty about not completing his university degree course; about not taking an active interest in local politics; about driving a motor car that drinks petrol with an almost uncontrollable thirst; about not buying a better car; about playing golf on Sundays; about not having thought enough about life insurance; about having forgotten to get the car cleaned; about missing school to go fishing at the age of eight; about eating too much unwholesome food and failing to exercise properly; about not buying his wife a better car; about having sexual fantasies about the well-built temporary typist in the company pool; about cheating a little on his income tax; about telling the assistant at the local fast food restaurant that he'd eat his hamburger outside and then eating it inside without paying the necessary tax; about encouraging his Catholic wife to take the contraceptive pill for seven years; and about actually thinking about encouraging her to have an abortion when she missed a period and they both thought she was pregnant.

That's a lot of guilt and there is a great deal of hidden agony in that mass of disconnected thoughts. At first sight it may seem that all those guilty feelings have nothing much in common. In fact they do have one very important common factor: they are all responses to the demands and teachings of those in our society who I shall call the guilt-makers.

The power of the priest

It is difficult to over estimate the power of the priest today. It should perhaps suffice to say that religious teachings are almost certainly the most important source of guilt in our society. I think it is also important to point out that although the more established, better organized religions have greater authority the size and age of a religious group do not necessarily have any bearing on the effectiveness of that religion as a guilt-making force.

While it is perfectly true, for example, that the Roman Catholic Church with its enormous membership and well respected hierachy has a great influence over its members and undoubtedly produces a good deal of guilt, there are smaller and far less well organized groups, describing themselves as religious organizations, which have a far more dramatic effect on their members.

Of all the religious teachings around the world the single group of instructions which cause the greatest amount of guilt are probably the ten commandments. They are simple enough and straightforward enough but they are also packed with negative advice which very few of us can claim to have followed to the letter. Indeed it is difficult to see just how anyone can hope to obey all ten commandments faithfully.

Consider the plight of an old, arthritic churchgoer who wants to attend church on Sunday to worship her God. If the church is too far away for her to walk then she must employ some sort of transport. But if she catches a bus or takes a taxi then she is encouraging someone to work and therefore to break one of the commandments. By fulfilling her obligation she is ensuring that someone else cannot. And just how many honest people can put their hands on their hearts and swear that they have never admired a smart motor car, a good piece of furniture, a magnificent house or a beautiful painting? How far is admiration from envy? What about soldiers in time of war? What right does the Church have to encourage its own members to break the commandment that forbids the taking of life?

These are real dilemmas which face real people and produce very real guilt.

The ten commandments apart, the teachings which

probably cause more guilt than any other are those which concern and surround the subject of conception.

There are around the world millions of women who must struggle with their consciences every month as they attempt to cope with their own desires, their husbands' desires and the teachings of their religious leaders. If they accept the ruling that all forms of contraception are an offence in God's eyes then they should only enjoy sexual intercourse as a prelude to a possible conception and another addition to the family. But at the same time the careful thinking parent will acknowledge that the world is rapidly becoming over-populated. There is no doubt that food is running out and that we're heading for a major shortage of all natural resources.

What does the careful, conscientious woman do? Does she accept the teachings of her church and have a large family or does she accept the teachings of her Government and have a small family? Or does she simply shower in cold water and push her husband away when he comes near her?

Abortion too is a cause of much guilt. The arguments about whether or not abortion is ever justified seem to go on for ever. Is a woman entitled to have a pregnancy terminated if she is dying? Does she have a right to have a pregnancy terminated if she knows that the baby she is carrying will be born badly deformed? Does she have a right to a termination if she is a victim of a rape attack?

Put at its bleakest does a 14-year-old mentally retarded girl with diabetes who is a rape victim and is carrying a deformed and badly malformed baby have a right to an abortion? And if she doesn't by what authority do those around her have the right to insist that she goes through with the pregnancy?

Those women who have fought their own consciences and decided to have abortions are often positively encouraged to feel guilty afterwards. The confessional box offers relief to some but total absolution is difficult to achieve in a society where guilt is a way of life.

Contraception and abortion are just two of the simplest and most straightforward problems faced by those whose lives are influenced in some real way by religious authority. For others there are far more complex issues and even more destructive problems to face.

If we sometimes find it difficult to believe that God intended religious celebrations to be such solemn and joyless occasions and worship to be such a painful experience we should perhaps remember that it was religious leaders who first discovered the power of guilt as a force.

Modern scientists who have studied brainwashing techniques believe that the individual who is obsessed with guilt is far easier to control than other individuals. Religious leaders have, however, known and taken advantage of this psychological fact for centuries, using guilt to keep their flocks under control and creating a range of demands which no one can ever hope to meet in order to ensure that all members of the church must feel guilty all the time. For all those who take their religion seriously guilt must be an inevitable unavoidable consequence.

The child is father of the man

Wordsworth knew what he was talking about when he wrote that line. He expressed a philosophy which has for centuries been understood and taken advantage of by organizations of many kinds.

It is, for example, not simply for philanthropic reasons that so many religious groups have organized schools. The truth is that the child's mind is easy to infiltrate. Schoolteachers have a tremendous opportunity to mould their charges, and the child who is taught religious principles at an early age will grow up with those principles fixed in his memory. Any attempts he may make to break away from the teachings to which he has been exposed are bound to result in the development of guilt feelings.

Even in schools where pupils aren't deliberately indoctrinated individual school teachers have a tremendous amount of power. Their own political and social prejudices are bound to rub off on their charges with the result that in later life attitudes and responses which may seem to conflict with those early impressions will produce feelings of great guilt.

The most manipulative teachers can, of course, intimidate and produce great fear in the developing and immature minds over which they have so much control. But in many ways it is not the obviously manipulative schoolteachers who have the greatest effect. The schoolteacher who bluntly tried to pass on his own prejudices may well produce so much opposition in the children in his care that they will grow up with feelings which bear no resemblance to his own.

For example, the teacher who is an ardent and enthusiastic atheist may overstate his case so vividly that many of the children who pass through his hands develop into enthusiastic churchgoers. It is, on the contrary, the gentle, popular teacher who will have the greatest effect and whose own personal principles and prejudices are most likely to have a lasting influence on the children he or she teaches. What happens is simply that the child grows up believing that the feelings expressed and the principles implied by that school teacher are the right ones.

If the school teacher is an ardent nonsmoker who carefully opens the classroom window when a smoking teacher has been in the room, the children who like him or her may grow up to share that particular prejudice. Moral principles, social behaviour and political attitudes can be passed on just as easily and as permanently as the rudiments of mathematics and English grammar.

The most effective and influential school teacher I ever met was a modest, delicate young woman whose quiet

36

voice and shy demeanour belied her effectiveness as a member of her chosen profession. She was a dedicated vegetarian and an opponent of all kinds of vivisection but she took care not to force her beliefs on to any of us. She was, however, so popular in a quiet and gentle sort of way that everyone who came into contact with her would eventually begin to feel guilty about eating meat. Naturally we also all developed an intense hatred of all forms of cruelty to animals.

By the time I left school most of those who had been taught by her had at the very least a deep sympathy for the causes she espoused. Several had actually become vegetarians much to the surprise and bemusement of their meat-eating parents. Ironically she, like other popular school teachers, had one other effect on her pupils. She introduced a sense of guilt in those children who failed to fulfil what seemed to be expected of them.

This type of guilt is common enough between children and demanding parents who openly expect a great deal from their offspring but it is not so common between children and their school teachers. Incidentally, it isn't confined to academic success or failure—many children feel that they have failed (and so feel guilty) if their sporting achievements don't match up to standards which they feel have been set.

Naturally, it isn't just our school teachers who fill us with their prejudices and pass on their own fears and hopes. We remain susceptible to the attitudes and opinions of experts throughout our lives. Paradoxically, the more civilized the community and the more intelligent and better educated we are the greater the chance of us being exposed to guilt-producing feelings. Consequently it is the more intelligent and better educated members of the community who are most likely to be aware of their obligations to those around them and the demands, rights and expectations of others. Broadly speaking the better educated we are the greater

37

the risk of feeling guilty.

Whatever occupation we may follow and whatever our role in life may be there will be no shortage of experts eager to tell us what we should and should not do and to imbue us with a sense of guilt should we dare to disobey their instructions. There are, for example, always doctors ready and willing to tell us what we should eat, what we should drink, what we should weigh, and what we should avoid.

There are plenty of psychologists happy to tell us what we should do to keep our marriages whole, our children happy, our relatives comfortable and our relationships strong. Should we fail to follow their advice and find ourselves in trouble of any kind then in theory we have only ourselves to blame.

Sadly, since no two experts seem to offer advice that doesn't conflict it is rarely possible to obey the dictates of all the experts at the same time. Guilt is, it seems, an inescapable consequence of all kinds of study.

Dirty books and bad habits

There is no internal conflict as great as that between our natural sexual desires and what we recognize as being socially acceptable sexual behaviour. For a variety of reasons most of us grew up with a sneaking suspicion that anything to do with sex must be rather dirty, nasty and unacceptable. Consequently when we become aware of our personal desires, our deeply-rooted fantasies and our physical expectations we suffer enormous feelings of guilt.

Rightly or wrongly sexual guilt is by no means confined to rapists, philanderers and adulterers. You can see feelings of sexual guilt being built all around you. Look around next time you're on the beach and you'll see small children changing into swimming costumes and struggling to hide their tiny bodies behind inadequate towels. A quick flash of thigh or bottom and they grab for the towel. If they don't do it themselves (because they haven't yet learned just how important it is to avoid such excesses of the flesh) then mother does it for them.

Is it any wonder that as a result of this type of repressive behaviour many people feel guilty either if they themselves accidentally expose too much flesh or if they accidentally or deliberately catch sight of someone else exposing flesh?

The guilt is made worse by the fact that although we have been taught that it is wrong to look at other people's naked bodies or to expose our own to other people many of us like looking at naked bodies. It is a natural part of the human sexual drive to show some interest in the unclothed forms of other members of our own species. And yet simple nudity produces so much guilt and so much agony that it is difficult to know where to start when describing the problems which exist.

There are, for example, many women who have never allowed their husbands to view them in the nude. They undress in the bathroom or with the bedroom lights switched off and they slide into bed quickly and carefully so that their husbands won't see anything they shouldn't see. If the bathroom door is accidentally left unlocked or the bedroom light switched on by accident they suffer agonies.

There are those who are so bewildered by their own conflict that they will take extraordinary steps to catch a glimpse of someone of the opposite sex and then proceed to complain about the fact that they have seen something they shouldn't have seen. The story about the old lady who complains that if she stands on a chair and leans on the wardrobe she can see the man next door undressing isn't apocryphal. It's common. And so very, very sad.

Many people who suffer damaging and painful feelings of guilt as a result of the conflict between their basic inner feelings and desires and their learned appreciation of what is socially acceptable in sexual terms react by over-reacting. Torn apart by the guilt they feel for their own sexual fantasies and physical needs they become enthusiastic opponents of anything which can be considered part of the great sexual revolution. Any sexual activity which they themselves find remotely attractive they condemn since only by condemning can they appease their own feelings of guilt.

Those haughty rather pompous individuals who object so strenuously when a pair of breasts are allowed to swing across a television screen or when a strip club owner puts advertising photographs outside his establishment are often reacting so violently simply because they themselves find it impossible to deal comfortably with their own sexual feelings. Because they were brought up to feel offended when confronted by nudity they feel guilty when they find that they enjoy such sights. And because they were brought up to regard sex as something rather disgraceful they are overwhelmed with guilt if they find that they actually enjoy it. Their repressive behaviour is built on their own guilt. Ironically and sadly it is these over enthusiastic opponents of things sexual who themselves are often guilty of the most hideous and fearsome sexual crimes.

The owners of clubs and cinemas which specialize in offering sexually exciting entertainment know very well that their most regular customers are often men who are regarded by their friends and relatives as prim, proper and rather straight-laced. Prostitutes recognize that the customers most likely to make outrageous demands or to offer dangerous violence are the men who reek of respectability and who seem almost sanctimonious in their outlook.

These people are all desperately afraid of their own sexual needs and are always extremely reluctant to admit to such needs. They are frightened because of an immensely powerful inner sense of guilt. Their aggressive denouncements of the indiscretions of others are simply a disguise for their own repressed urges. When their disguise breaks down they sometimes become sexual criminals, often choosing as victims those whom they regard as having contributed to the breakdown of sexual mores in the country at large.

Fortunately, it is only a small proportion of those who fight against all forms of sexual freedom who actually resort to violence. The number of Rippers is thankfully few. The majority of these individuals assuage their guilt by campaigning ferociously against all things sexual. As self appointed curators of public taste they help to maintain the structure of a repressive society which will lead to the development of yet another generation of guilt-ridden individuals. It is they who perpetuate the agonies of sexual guilt and who ensure that even in our so called 'permissive society' there are not only many thousands who are overwhelmed with sexual guilt but there are many more who feel guilty because they don't feel guilty.

Modern pressures

Many of the social and cultural expectations which are the basis for our feelings of guilt have evolved over many hundreds of years. Religious teachings which provide so many of us with so much guilt have been gradually improved and expanded for centuries. There are, nevertheless, many modern pressures which have just as dramatic an effect on our lives and which help to produce equally damaging types of guilt.

I've already mentioned the women's liberation movement and I've no intention of taking sides on this touchy subject but whether you are in favour of the emancipation of women or totally opposed to the principle does cause a great deal of guilt today, affecting both men and women.

Many of the other guilt-making influences which are most troublesome in our modern society concern the elderly. Modern medical techniques have helped increase life expectations dramatically and there are today very many

41

thousands of people alive in their seventies, eighties and nineties who need looking after.

Unfortunately, the improvements in the quality of medical care have not been matched by equivalent improvements in the quality of community care. This means that there are just not enough hospital beds, old people's homes or special accomodation for all those elderly people. Inevitably the problems of looking after them has to be faced by younger relatives who may themselves have overwhelming responsibilities.

The circumstances which lead directly to the development of guilt among younger relatives are well enough established. One elderly partner dies and the remaining partner is no longer capable of looking after himself or herself alone. There are no community care facilities and so the old person's doctors or whichever social workers have been given the responsibility for dealing with the individual will call on the relatives for help.

It isn't easy for a young couple to turn away an aged relative even if they themselves have only a small home, more than enough children and problems enough to put a strain on any marriage. And in circumstances like that whatever happens will produce enormous feelings of guilt. The woman who turns away her mother-in-law will be full of guilt. But on the other hand the same will be true of the woman who takes her mother-in-law into her own home and sees her children and her marriage suffer. The professionals in our society who make these demands on individual families, often as though speaking on behalf of society itself, can and frequently do create absolute havoc.

Medical advances have added to the reservoir of potential guilt in our society in many other ways too. It is now possible to perform many life saving operations on infants who might otherwise have died. In many instances the infant saved will live an entirely abnormal life, being physically paralysed and mentally disabled. I don't intend to try and answer the questions this type of problem raises but it is important to understand that whatever answers are chosen in whatever circumstances the end result is very likely to be the development of a good deal of guilt.

The young parents who decide that they should not allow their child to be subject to an operation that may extend the quantity of its life but may also be unlikely to offer much in the way of quality will feel guilty when their baby dies. They'll have to ask themselves whether they were right to allow that child to die and then they'll have to live with their decision.

On the other hand the parents who decide that they should allow surgeons to operate may well find their whole future bound up with looking after a physically and mentally disabled child. Sometimes the disabilities can be frightening and the consequences for a marriage unbearable. In those circumstances if one partner pressed for the operation he or she will undoubtedly feel guilty as the marriage crumbles.

Guilt is a common consequence of unemployment too. The steadily rising rate of unemployment undoubtedly means that many men in their forties and fifties will never work again. For men who have been brought up to believe that work is an essential part of life such a burden can be unbearable. Like many doctors I have had to deal with a large number of men who have lost their jobs. Almost all of them have been wracked with guilt for in their own eyes they have failed to fulfil their obligations to their families.

Mr Porter was a fairly typical example of a man in his mid-forties who had suddenly lost his job. He'd been brought up to believe that it is a man's duty to go off to work each morning, return home each evening, preferably with his hands dirty, and collect a pay packet on Friday.

When he was made redundant he simply couldn't face telling his wife. For four days he went out to work, dirtied his hands, ate his packed lunch and returned home in the evening. Then when on Friday he didn't have a pay packet to take home with him he tried to kill himself. Fortunately there was a train strike that day and Mr Porter was found lying on the railway lines with a handful of pills in his stomach and the morning express train stranded a hundred miles away.

Mr Porter, like so many other men in similar situations had no reason to fear for the future. He had a good sum of redundancy money due to him and his wife still had a part-time job. Their children had left home and their needs were fairly simple. Their house was paid for and they owned their own car. He, however, had been unable to cope with the guilt he felt for having no job. To him redundancy meant failure as a man and it was a failure that he just couldn't cope with. No one told him that the rules had changed, that society had progressed and that the working man's ethic was no longer valid.

Many people brought up in the days of the soup kitchens and the charity hand-out find the many varieties of social security payment difficult to accept. It is said that the number of people who fail to claim money due to them far exceeds the number of people claiming money that isn't due to them. By and large the individuals who don't claim money fail to do so because they consider all Government handouts to be a form of charity. They don't accept that they are only receiving money to which they are entitled. On the contrary they believe that if they need to take public money thay have failed both as people and as members of that society. Even though the money is theirs by right, if they take it they feel guilty.

As the years pass by and life gets more and more complicated so it seems that the sources of guilt in our society become more varied and more numerous.

If he loves you he'll buy you a diamond

The commercial pressures which exist in our society are enormous, far reaching and too numerous to count. From the moment we get up in the morning to the time we go to bed at night we are subjected to an endless series of pressures. In the morning post there are circulars from mail order companies and publishers selling magazine subscriptions and books. We learn before breakfast that if we fail to read such and such a magazine regularly we'll be failing ourselves and our family. We simply won't be well enough informed to survive in a world that is becoming increasingly competitive. And if we don't buy the right sort of encyclopaedia we'll be failing the children. Their educational chances will be ruined for the sake of a modest expenditure on a set of books.

The daily newspapers are stuffed with advertisements. There are people wanting to sell us soaps and perfumes to make us smell sweeter and banks wanting to lend us money so that we can buy better things for our families. There are motor car companies offering us faster, safer, more comfortable vehicles and there are wholesalers selling spectacular pieces of furniture at knockdown prices. If we don't buy those soaps and perfumes then we'll be going out into the world offending people with our own bodily smells. If we don't borrow the money we've been offered then we'll be depriving our families. If we don't buy the latest car then we'll be failing ourselves. And if we don't buy new furniture how will our families know how much we care?

The ride to work in the morning takes us past a whole series of hoardings and posters. We see that if we don't buy the children the right sort of breakfast cereal we'll be depriving them of essential vitamins and minerals. The implications are that they'll die of malnutrition simply because we selected the wrong breakfast cereal. If we don't buy locally we'll be failing fellow workers who need our custom in order to live. By buying from abroad we'll be putting our neighbours out of work, causing endless hardship and pain.

Should we fail to buy the right sort of after-shave lotion we'll be missing out and so will those close to us. The same goes for clothes. If we don't spend our money on buying the most fashionable and delectable clothes how can those close to us know that we respect and admire their taste? Surely they'll take it as just another personal insult if we expose them to the sight of our bodies draped in last years outfits?

At work there are other pressures and fresh guilts. Someone comes round with flags for a charity that is collecting money. If you fail to put something in the box then the charity will have less money to spend. The people who depend upon the charity will be deprived. Someone who is blind, deaf, disabled or suffering from cancer will suffer because of your refusal to spare a few pence.

The boss wants some overtime done and although you'd planned to go out with the family you know that you can't really refuse him. You know that if you refuse to do the overtime the factory may stand to lose a rather special order. The boss has put a lot of work into getting that order and he'll be deeply hurt if it falls through. Besides there are lots of other people who stand to make money out of the deal and they'll suffer if you make a fuss. Unfortunately, of course, whichever way you turn someone is going to be hurt. There is good cause for guilt either way. Stay at work and the family will suffer. Go home and the boss will suffer.

A supplier rings up with a sad story explaining why a delivery is late. He explains that if the order is cancelled he'll probably go bankrupt. You know that if the order isn't delivered soon your own factory is going to be in trouble with meeting its own commitments. Whatever you do is likely to produce feelings of guilt. If you give the supplier an ultimatum then he's going to be miserable. If you give him more time then your own factory may be damaged in some way.

On the way home there are shop window displays designed to catch the eye, the heart and the conscience of all who pass by. The slogans the window-dressers use are as clever as those the copywriters favour. In the jeweller's shop over a display of expensive rings you'll see signs like 'Does he love you enough to buy you a diamond?'

In the shoe shop you'll see posters telling you just how important it is that your children have shoes which fit their feet properly. The copywriter carefully uses phrases which explain just how much damage you can do if you buy cheap shoes or if you delay buying shoes for too long.

The health food shop will have jars and bottles galore explaining the virtues and values of their special products. They may not even knock more conventional foods. They don't need to. All they have to do is make it clear just how valuable natural foodstuffs are and just how much your children will benefit if they are fed the right sort of diet. Do you really want to gamble with your children's lives just to save a few pence?

The luxury shops will not hesitate to make it clear just how much your status will rise if you buy the right sort of TV video game, the right brand of camera or the right type of suitcases. Buy the wrong items and you'll be recognized by your neighbours as an ineffective failure with bad taste. Buy the right items and you can hold your head up high as a success. In the world of the super-sell social and economic failure is a justifiable cause of shame and guilt.

At home in the evening there are the usual range of advertisements on the television designed to make you feel guilty if you fail to respond. Don't you really owe it to the family to take them for a week's holiday in the sun somewhere? Doesn't your spouse deserve a week or two's break after a year's solid effort? And don't the children deserve a day out at that wonderful amusement park in the country?

Don't they deserve new bicycles? Don't they deserve new electronic toys? Shouldn't you feel guilty if you fail to provide them with all the things they want?

When you pick up a magazine you find that there are advertisements for a special type of life insurance. Shouldn't you really be making sure that your family is properly protected? Don't you owe it to them to buy them the best insurance possible? Surely you should feel guilty if you haven't thought about what will happen to them if something happens to you. And while you're thinking about money shouldn't you really be looking for a better paid job? Is it enough to have a job that is pleasant and pays fairly well? Or should we all look for the best paid employment and not expect to enjoy our work?

These guilt-provoking pressures really are endless. Advertisers of all kinds deliberately use our capacity for guilt to help sell their products. The copywriters know that if they can create sufficient feelings of guilt then we will succumb to their entreaties. And they know that they can make us feel guilty by suggesting to us that if we don't buy such and such an item or invest in this or that programme we are failing those who are nearest and dearest to us.

Many advertisers deliberately aim at children knowing that they can then rely on the children to do their work for them. The company which wants to sell sweets or chocolates will carefully try and captivate the interest of younger viewers or readers. They know very well that that's the best way to get mum to open her purse.

Commercial interests are among the most powerful and effective guilt makers.

5

The Influences of Guilt

Although there are very many causes of guilt, problems usually arise because we are persuaded, for one reason or another, to compare ourselves to others. That in itself would not necessarily be dangerous if it were not for the fact that we are comparing ourselves not with the realistic accomplishments, demands and expectations of others but with their entirely unrealistic accounts of what they expect from us.

It is almost inevitable that we should fail to come up to expectation when we compare our private selves with the ideals favoured by those around us. The truth is that when we are comparing our private view of ourselves with our public view of others we are bound to seem to fail while others are bound to appear to succeed.

Let's take a look at some of the causes of guilt that I have already outlined and see exactly what I mean. First, consider the ways in which personal relationships produce a feeling of guilt. When our parents expect us to behave in a particular way and we fail to do so we usually feel guilty because we feel we have let them down. We believe that we have failed to behave in the way that they would have behaved. They, therefore, have the right to feel aggrieved and we must inevitably feel guilty for having failed to behave in the appropriate manner.

But is that all entirely realistic? Did our parents always do everything that their parents wanted them to do? Did they put their own parents first? Of course they didn't. And so we are comparing ourselves not with a realistic example but with an idealized example. We are comparing ourselves not with what our parents themselves actually did but what they feel they ought to have done and consequently with what they would like us to do. Their own guilt feeling about the way they behaved towards their parents is helping to reinforce our own feelings of guilt.

It is perhaps even easier to describe what I mean by referring to the type of guilt we acquire as a result of social pressures from those around us. I've already described how it is that the individuals who themselves feel the greatest conflict between their own natural desires and what they themselves have been taught is right are most enthusiastic in their support for all kinds of laws and codes governing our behaviour. So we have a situation in which most of us find ourselves struggling to reconcile our private desires, ambitions and needs with the public desires, ambitions and needs of people whose own private desires, ambition and needs are no better than our own!

If you feel guilty when you stare at a good-looking member of the opposite sex walking down the street you feel guilty because of moral standards set by and supported by individuals who themselves feel guilty because they are painfully aware of their own desires when confronted by good-looking members of the opposite sex walking down the street.

Guilt is such a pervasive, overwhelming emotion that we are very rarely aware of all this. As our feelings of guilt rise and grow we gradually become more and more convinced that we alone are failing in our public and private responsibilities. We become convinced that our failure and our subsequent feeling of guilt is unique. It is this feeling of having failed those whose demands, expectations and hopes we respect most which does the damage. Whether we have failed those whom we regard as close to us in a personal way or we have failed those whom we regard as guardians of the collective social conscience we feel shame at our failure.

The woman who has married someone of whom her parents do not approve feels guilty because she has let them down and because she has failed to accede to their wishes. Shame is not far away. The woman who has been taking the contraceptive pill because she cannot cope with the thought of having any more children feels guilty for having succumbed to her natural desire for sex and for having failed to obey the dictates of those whom she regards as overseers of her religious conscience. Again it isn't difficult to see just how that guilt can be turned into shame and how that unhappy woman can begin to feel a failure and a very inferior being.

What makes all this so much worse is that we are usually quite unaware of the ways in which our guilt develops and totally unaware of the many ways in which the guilt we have acquired is likely to have an effect on our lives. Without our realizing it our lives and our actions are in fact being influenced and directed not by positive willpower but by unseen, unrecognized, unconscious mechanisms. Until we understand those mechanisms we cannot hope to control our own destinies.

Of all the effects which guilt has upon us the most damaging is undoubtedly the feeling of inferiority. We may not be fully aware of the fact that it is guilt which is influencing our lives but slowly we do become aware of the fact that we have done something of which we should feel ashamed.

Slowly as our guilt builds we begin to feel that if people really knew just what we were like they would have nothing at all to do with us. They would quite reasonably reject us out of hand if they knew what sort of people we were.

It is precisely that inferiority, that insecurity, that lack of confidence and that shame which make us stick to jobs we dislike, which make us unwilling to make changes which might affect our lives in any dramatic way, which make us envy people who seem better able to cope, which make us work too hard, which make us make quite unnecessary and immensely painful sacrifices, which make us deprive ourselves of all pleasures and which gradually deprive us of our own sense of identity, our own pride and our own ability to control our lives.

Feeling inferior

To describe just how guilt produces these feelings of inferiority and how inferiority affects our lives and influences our thoughts and deeds I want to tell you about a patient of mine.

When I first met him, Mr Roberts was 42 years old. For seven years he had been a manager of a local branch of a large chain of stores. The job gave him a good standard of living and a fair amount of responsibility. He had a large detached house in one of the best areas of the town, a wife with a good wardrobe, a car of her own and enough jewellery to merit a burglar alarm, and two teenage children at private schools.

I first met him because his wife had walked out on him and he came both for support and advice. His life was shattered and he really didn't understand what had happened or why his marriage had gone wrong. As far as he was concerned he had provided his family with everything they needed.

When we talked I found out that for several years he had been devoting himself almost entirely to the running of his store. Every weekday he got up at seven so that he could be in the store before anyone else. He told me that it was his responsibility to be there first to set a good example. He ate his lunch in his office and didn't leave in the evening until the last member of staff had gone home and the cleaners were busy working their way round the store. Indeed, on some occasions he even stayed in the store until the cleaners had finished their work. In some ways he considered himself to be the captain of a ship. He thought it was his duty to stay at his post long after everyone else had gone home.

That I suppose might have been acceptable if he'd left it there. But not even getting in earlier and leaving later than everyone else was enough for Mr Roberts. In the evening when he made his way home he took a briefcase full of buying orders, stock details and sales receipts. He took the latest catalogues and the latest trade journals and he spent hours crouched in his study leafing through these. He rarely got to bed before midnight and his wife saw him only when he popped into the kitchen to pick up his evening meal or a cup of coffee.

It was very much the same story at weekends. On Saturdays he would always go into the store just to make sure that everything was going all right. He would never leave before six or seven in the evening and even then he would usually pack his briefcase with another set of documents. Even Sundays were spent poring over more paperwork, puzzling over staff problems or working on proposed window displays. He found delegation impossible and much to the annoyance of his staff insisted on being shown every piece of paper relating to his store.

Although his family had been on holiday each year Mr Roberts himself hadn't been away for several years. He always found some problem that needed his personal attention. One year there had been a small fire in the stock room. Another year there had been a crisis when a departmental manageress had run off with the assistant buyer. And another year a spate of shoplifting by young school children had meant extra work for him.

He was, he readily admitted, a workaholic and his private life had suffered as a result. 'I used to play golf and go swimming quite regularly,' he told me, 'but I haven't done either of those for years now'.

More important, perhaps, he hadn't been out with his wife or his children for years. 'They don't seem to understand that I only do it all for them', he told me plaintively. 'I just want them to have security and everything they need.'

He hadn't realized that his family had needed him just as much as they'd needed financial security and material comforts.

When we talked I tried to understand exactly why he felt that he needed to work so hard. I asked him if his immediate superiors demanded too much of him. 'No, not at all,' he agreed. 'In fact they're always telling me to take more time off.' Rather ashamedly he admitted to me that he had in fact had a good deal of trouble with his staff because of his inability to delegate. 'They seem to feel that I should let them have more responsibility,' he explained, 'but I'm just frightened that something is going to go wrong. I have to keep an eye on everything.' When I asked him if he'd had staff problems in the past or if he had ever been let down he admitted that he hadn't.

It wasn't until the third meeting we had that Mr Roberts slowly began to unwind and tell me enough about his life for the source of his inability to relax to become apparent. And when we finally did uncover the root of the problem Mr Roberts could hardly believe that he hadn't realized what was happening.

Back in his late twenties he had worked for a large manufacturing company as a sales representative. He had been married for no more than two or three years when he had suddenly been made redundant. Talking to him I couldn't see any reason why he might consider that he had been responsible for his own dismissal. It seemed that the company for which he worked was simply going through a bad patch and laying off employees. Mr Roberts, being one of the younger employees was dismissed on the usual 'last in—first out' basis.

For eighteen months he had been without a job, and that period of unemployment had left a scar on his mind that had continued to affect his whole attitude to life. While he was unemployed he had seen his wife forced to go out to work in a local factory to earn some money. He'd seen his children dressed in clothes bought from local jumble sales. He'd seen his family living on a diet of nothing much more than the cheapest available forms of carbohydrate. And he'd felt guilty and ashamed of all that.

The guilt and the shame had made him feel inferior and very insecure. Even when he'd got a good, safe job he still unconsciously felt guilty for those bad days. And always at the back of his mind was the feeling that it might happen again if he wasn't careful. Slowly during the years of plenty the insecurity and the fear grew. He began to feel guilty if he took time off from work to play golf or to go swimming because he couldn't help thinking that he ought to be concentrating on making sure that the future remained safe and secure.

The burden of guilt that Mr Roberts had carried had gradually begun to ruin his whole life and to affect the very relationships which had inspired the guilt in the first place. Of course, even when he had recognized all this Mr Roberts still didn't find it easy to start controlling his life, but he found it easier. He was at last able to understand why he felt so anxious to look after his store and he was able to distinguish between those actions which could be considered reasonable and those which were unreasonable.

He recognized, at last, that he wouldn't be putting his job at risk if he delegated a little more; if he allowed the cleaners to do their job without his supervision; and if he allowed the buyers and department heads to look after their own problems. With his guilt uncovered and the subsequent sense of inferiority and insecurity laid bare he began to find time to enjoy his life a little more. His wife, who had never wanted to leave him in the first place, returned home full of renewed enthusiasm for the future.

The number of ways in which guilt can affect us is matched only by the potential number of sources. Guilt doesn't only produce inferiority, insecurity and shame, it can also be responsible for the eventual development of such

emotional hang-ups as self-pity. The original guilt can easily be hidden in a whole sequence of mental traumas which
make the simple phrase 'guilt complex' seem unbelievably
trite. Guilt can often be the prime cause of many serious
mental disorders which might otherwise be regarded as
having no obvious cause.

Depression is a disease which doctors commonly try to
tie up to some specific event in the patient's life. After all
there is nothing exceptional about a woman who has lost
her husband becoming depressed. That is perfectly under-
standable and although the patient may need treatment the
outlook will be considered bright. Similarly a man who has
lost his job and become depressed will not be considered
unusual in any way. And nor would an individual who had
suffered some severe financial loss be considered mentally
unstable if depression followed.

If Mr Roberts the store manager had become depressed
it would have been difficult for anyone to see any immediate cause for his depression. After all in purely practical,
superficial terms he had nothing to be depressed about. He
had a good job, a wife and two healthy children, and a fine
home. Why should he feel depressed? Under those circumstances he might well be thought to have acquired his
depression as a result of some biochemical abnormality or
some inherited susceptibility to mental illness. And the
treatment would accordingly be designed to treat that type
of deep-rooted cause. But as we have already seen, Mr
Roberts's problems all stemmed from a well hidden feeling
of guilt. A feeling which could easily be overlooked if Mr
Roberts hadn't been prepared to look into his past and
search for potential sources of guilt.

Let me make a plea to everyone who has either suffered
or knows someone who has suffered from a serious depression. Do please remember that although a drug prescription may disguise the symptoms of depression; may
give the diminishing appetite a much needed boost; may

solve the problem of sleeplessness; and may soothe the troubled nerves a little, it will not solve the problem of the depression itself if any underlying guilt remains intact.

Guilt is an all pervasive, ever present emotion which affects all our lives in many different ways. It should never be underestimated as a potential source of distress and where there is any mental illness, however minor or however serious, guilt as a cause should always be sought and if possible exposed to the harsh light of a realistic examination.

The physical damage that guilt can do

Since I have now shown just how guilt can produce all sorts of mental traumas and since it is already well established that there are strong links between mental stresses and physical disorders it isn't difficult to realize that there must also be a link between guilt and many physical illnesses.

Consider Mr Godber. Anyone who knew him would be convinced that he had nothing at all to fear, nothing to be ashamed about and nothing to regret. He had in the space of half a life time built up a massive chain of shoe shops which together enabled him to enjoy a life style which most of us only ever read about.

He had begun his business career at the age of 21 with a few pounds left to him by an uncle. With that money he'd bought a few hundred pairs of shoes that had been salvaged from a fire in a large store and he'd hired a market stall. The shoes had been sold off quite quickly at a decent profit and the young businessman had then moved into a small shop in a precinct of a growing industrial town.

By the age of 30 Mr Godber had twelve shops, a turnover of hundreds of thousands of pounds a year, a villa in the South of France, a large apartment in London, a Rolls Royce, a Ferrari, and a failed marriage. For some that might have been enough. For Mr Godber it was just a beginning. Another five years later he had doubled his number of shops, tripled his annual turnover and quadrupled his profits. An island in the Carribean had been added to the villa and the apartment, and a bank acount in Switzerland allowed to grow to comfortable proportions.

After his first attack of angina at the age of 37 he stopped work for a month and then opened three more shops and a restaurant in Scotland. No one was really surprised when, six months later he had his first heart attack. He had after all been living at a pace that few people could have managed to stand. I first saw him six weeks after he had been discharged from hospital after that first heart attack. He was still at home, in theory convalescing. In practice he was working on plans for a second restaurant, preparing to build an ocean going yacht which he intended to turn into a floating gambling casino and making preliminary arrangements for the building of his own shoe factory.

He readily admitted that he didn't need to earn any more money. His Swiss bank account alone contained enough wealth for him to live comfortably for the rest of his life. But despite the fact that his working habits had endangered his life and would probably prove his eventual downfall he couldn't stop himself. He had to keep working.

I asked him what he was trying to prove and who he thought he needed to impress. Angrily he told me that he wasn't trying to prove anything and that he certainly didn't need to impress anyone. He told me exactly how much money he had made and just how much power he had. When he'd finished I waited a few moments without saying anything.

'My father,' he admitted eventually. 'I suppose I'm still trying to please my father.' Gradually he told me how when he'd been a boy his father had always wanted him to do well. At junior school if he didn't come top in his class his father had never been angry, just disappointed.

'He'd just look very sad and go off into the living room

with a book,' he remembered. 'It hurt me more than if he'd hammered the life out of me with a slipper. It made me more and more determined to please him. I just remember feeling so guilty every time I came home if I couldn't please him. The fact that he seemed so miserable if I didn't succeed made me feel awful.'

Even when his father died Mr Godber had continued to try harder all the time. Even when he had made his first million he felt he still had to do better in order to satisfy his father. However successful he became he could still see the face of the man he loved full of disappointment and despair.

Mr Godber died two weeks before his fortieth birthday. Despite the warnings of everyone around him he'd insisted on travelling to America to fix up a deal with the supplier of some machinery. He died a dissatisfied multi-millionaire; killed by his own attempts to satisfy his father.

The guilt he felt every time he failed to win approval from his father had turned him into an incurable workaholic.

In many cases the link between guilt and physical illness is not so easy to identify. When that is the case it is perhaps more realistic to look first of all for a general link between the mind and the body and then to look for the type of guilt most likely to have produced the stresses and strains producing the illness concerned.

The list of physical illnesses now accepted as being caused by stress and strain of one sort or another is now extremely long. Chest pains, indigestion, heart disease, stomach ulcers, palpitations, asthma, diarrhoea, backache, skin conditions of many kinds, breathlessness and so on are just a few of the specific disorders recognized as having a powerful link with the mind. In addition general feelings of tiredness and malaise are also commonly associated with disorders of the mind.

Although it is perfectly true that many external factors

are responsible for the types of stress which produce disease it is also true that internal problems are often responsible. And even where mental stress is not alone responsible it is often part of a general state of affairs responsible both for the development of specific symptoms and for a general susceptibility to physical illness.

Whenever there is a link established between stress and physical illness then guilt must always be considered as a primary source of mental stress.

The good points

So far I've discussed only the negative influences of guilt. It is, however, important to realize that not all guilt is destructive and that there are some consolations!

To begin with, of course, it is important for us all to remember that guilt is an entirely normal and sometimes healthy human response. In some circumstances it is right that we should feel guilty. To that extent guilt is an important and useful restraining device without which there would be no chance of our developing personal or community relationships.

Without the threat of guilt and all the consequent agonies there would be much less to deter us from crimes of all kinds. It is, after all, the restraint offered by our personal consciences as much as the threats offered by the courts which ensure that the majority of us obey the laws of the land.

In addition it is important that we remember that guilt can be an effective and powerful driving force capable of leading us to success in many different walks of life. It is guilt and the fears associated with guilt which keep most of us honest and conscientious. Guilt is also one of the driving forces which helps make us careful, moral, kind, generous, ambitious, hard-working and most creative. Those who fear guilt the most frequently turn out to be kindest, fairest and most thoughtful. Those who have to contend with guilt cannot afford to be anything else if they are to wrestle successfully with their inner consciences. External criticism is as nothing compared to the criticism we offer ourselves.

Many of the most successful people who have ever lived have been riddled with guilt. Some, it is true, have suffered a great deal as well as a result of their susceptibility to guilt. There have been others, however, just as successful who have managed to harness their guilt and keep it under control.

We can now move on to learn how best we can harness and use our own guilt. I will describe how you can recognize guilt as a potential asset and how you can learn to use your own guilt instead of allowing it to destroy you. Once you have learned to minimize your susceptibility to guilt and make the most of it you will not only be able to cope with life far more effectively but you will also be far better equipped to take your life into your own hands.

6

Coping with Guilt

Before we can do anything about our feelings of guilt we must understand where they come from and learn something about the mechanisms which are responsible for their development. First of all let's go back to the type of guilt which we acquire from our personal relationships.

Parents

Most of us acquire a good deal of our guilt from our relationships with our parents. They are, after all, the people with whom most of us have our earliest and closest relationships. It is important to understand that I'm not suggesting that parents are universally evil or that they spend days struggling to devise ways in which they can force their offspring to feel guilty. That would, of course, be nonsensical. What I am suggesting is that whether or not they are aware of it, and whatever their motives may be, all parents must at some time or another produce feelings of guilt in their children by the very fact that they love and respect them, have ambitions for them and so on. The greater the love, the closer the bonds, the more intense that feeling of guilt is likely to be. It is, of course, perfectly true that domineering parents will produce feelings of guilt and that aggressive, over-demanding parents may deliberately use guilt as a weapon. But in the majority of cases guilt develops slowly, insidiously and probably unnoticed both by parents and by children.

To identify the existence of guilt it is not only necessary for us to take a long close look at the nature and form of our relationships but also necessary for us to spend some time examining our own motives. Guilt can have a tremendous influence on the way that we behave and by looking at the things we do and trying to decide why we do them it is sometimes possible to identify guilt as a driving force in our lives when we might not otherwise be aware of its existence.

If, for example, you ask yourself why you always go and visit your parents on a Sunday, why you always invite them over for the New Year celebrations or why you always invite them for Christmas, you may find that you are doing these things not through any conscious desire but because you'll feel guilty if you don't.

The next question to be asked is why will you feel guilty if you don't do any of these things? Is it because of something your parents have said or implied or is it because you think that their feelings will be hurt if you don't behave in this way? Do you feel that they'll be disappointed if you don't make your Sunday pilgrimage or your Christmas trip? Or have they made it clear that they expect you to behave in this way and that if you don't they'll feel let down?

By asking these questions we can see how easy it is for our lives to be influenced by guilt without our really being aware of it.

Friends

Take a look at your relationships with some of your closest friends. If you meet regularly for coffee or drinks in the pub do you meet because you positively want to or because you feel you ought to? If you always go on holiday with another couple do you do so because that's really how you like to spend your holiday or is it because you don't want to hurt their feelings by making alternative arrangements? If you always go on shopping trips with a friend is it because you like shopping that way or because you'll feel bad about it if you don't?

The two magic words which really give away the extent

of your guilt, are 'ought to'. How often have you used them when talking about friends and relatives? You'll hear them all the time if you listen to people's idle chatter.

'We ought to invite the Browns round to dinner. It's our turn to have them over.'

'I ought to ring George. He's left three messages for me at the office.'

'We ought to take your mother out this weekend.'

'If we're inviting Fred and Sheila then we ought to invite Jim and Glenda.'

'I ought to send the Youngs a card. We got one from them.'

'We ought to get the house painted. Everyone else in the street has had theirs done.'

'You ought to write to your Aunt Thelma. She'll wonder what has happened if you don't.'

'We ought to get the children new bikes for Christmas.'

In all these situations guilt is the driving force. It's guilt that is making us do things and guilt that makes us feel bad if we don't. It is there playing an important part in all our close relationships; whether they be relatives, friends or lovers.

I am not suggesting that we should always refuse to do anything that we're influenced to do by guilt, but I do suggest that we should realize and acknowledge the existence of guilt within our relationships. It is much healthier for guilt to be acknowledged as a driving force than for it to be allowed to remain hidden and unrecognized.

By analysing our relationships a little, and by learning to understand precisely why we do what we do then it is possible to preserve and indeed strengthen those relationships. If we are to enjoy love and friendship then we have to be prepared to make sacrifices and on occasions to do things that we don't really want to do. However, the danger, both to ourselves and to the existence of those relationships, of guilt producing such unwanted side effects as envy, jealousy, fear, hatred or contempt can be drastically reduced by bringing the guilt out into the open rather than letting it smoulder unnoticed.

Before we finish with personal relationships and guilt I must make one more extremely important point. We must none of us forget that just as we can all be influenced by guilt produced by our relationships with others so we can all influence others by making them feel guilty. It is, therefore, important not only that we be aware of the existence and influence of guilt on our own actions but that we also be aware of the many ways in which our own behaviour may produce guilt in others. Guilt is very much a two-edged weapon. We are all as likely to produce it in others as we are to suffer ourselves.

Society

Just as we all worry a great deal about what our friends and relations think so we all worry a great deal about our role and responsibility in society. The amount of guilt we suffer as a result of our attempts to satisfy the expectations of those who make the rules is incalculable.

Political, religious, social and commercial pressures all mix together to push us first in one direction and then in another. We are manipulated, often deliberately but sometimes accidentally, by people we have never met who may themselves be influenced by their own guilt and by their own guilt-induced feelings of inferiority or insecurity.

There are indeed so many influencing forces about in our society today that it is no easy matter to decide just who is forcing us to do what. But with a little thought and deliberation it should be possible to begin to analyse the influences and to begin to see just how those separate forces have an effect on our lives.

For a great many of us religion is the most powerful, most dramatic force in our lives. For millions of people around the world guilt is inspired by theories and doctrines produced either by mythical figures long since dead or by people living in a world quite different to the one in which they themselves must live. In those circumstances guilt is as inevitable as sin.

As we struggle to deal with these guilty feelings most of us must also learn to cope with the many varied guilts produced by a commercial world which has an entirely different set of values and which makes an entirely different series of demands upon us.

It is hardly surprising that in circumstances like this the incidence of stress diseases rises annually, the number of people requiring psychiatric care goes up almost monthly and the consumption of tranquillisers and other drugs rockets upwards, quite out of control.

In a world where we are all continually being bombarded by demands, instructions, pleas, suggestions and exhortations, failure is unavoidable. There is no way that we can hope to satisfy all those who would like us to behave in some particular way. The only hope is to try and differentiate between the many and varied demands, to identify those producing guilt and to make a conscious effort to limit our susceptibility. Identifying guilt-producing pressures is perhaps best done not by looking for the causes of guilt (which are often disguised and difficult to appreciate) but by looking at our attitudes, beliefs and behavioural patterns and trying to decide why we do what we do.

Often it doesn't take long to find a guilt-producing influence. The woman who refuses to take the contraceptive pill because her religious mentors disapprove but who then feels guilty about having to turn her husband away at unsuitable times of the month will know without much thought the source of that particular type of guilt. On the other hand things are not always that obvious. The man who feels that he ought to buy a new car may not immediately be aware of the reasons behind the guilt he feels when he doesn't rush round to the garage and put in his order. It may be that he feels guilty because he's letting down the family. He may feel that he's not doing his best for them by expecting them to sit in a three-year-old model. He may simply feel that he isn't doing his bit for the ailing car industry or that he isn't doing his bit to keep the economy going. He may on the other hand feel that he has let himself down. He may be convinced that by not buying the latest and most extravagantly equipped motor car he is putting his family at risk. The possibilities are endless.

By establishing the reasons behind his beliefs and the reasons for the guilt he feels; by looking behind his hopes, fears and aspirations for the motivating forces he will be far better able to understand the pressures he is under. And then, with that understanding as a basis, he will be far better equipped to deal with this type of guilt.

He will be able to decide for himself on a conscious, rational level whether or not he wants his life to be ruled by the car industry, the politicians or the expectations of neighbours he doesn't know. By isolating the sources of his guilt he will be in a good position to minimize the damage that guilt can do.

Build up your own defences

Identifying sources and causes of guilt is one important way to minimize the damage that is done. It is also important to be aware that by building up our own defences we will be better equipped to deal with guilt-provoking forces. One of the indisputable facts about guilt is that the people who are most susceptible are the people who have little faith in their own strengths and abilities and little in the way of confidence or self-assurance.

Timid, shy, self-conscious individuals are often the very people who are most likely to suffer from guilt for the very reason that by and large their timidity and uncertainty will itself usually be a consequence of unconsciously acquired guilt. Guilt and uncertainty go together like beef and mustard. The two forces are closely linked in such a way that each will build on the other. Guilt produces uncertainty which produces a susceptibility to guilt which produces uncertainty and so on and so on.

Breaking the cycle, getting out of the vicious circle defined by these two forces, can only be done by eradicating some of that self-consciousness and replacing it with a little self-confidence and self assurance. And that is a task which sounds far more of a problem that it truly is. For the undeniable, indisputable truth is that those who suffer most from guilt and who are most susceptible to guilt *do* have a great deal to be proud about.

Because of their awareness of the needs and expectations of others they tend to be remarkably kind and gentle people, more honest than most, harder working and more ambitious that individuals who are less susceptible to guilt, and invariably both thoughtful and appreciative. If you are one of those individuals who are most susceptible to guilt then you should try to rebuild your personal defences by listing your own good points.

Just sit down with a piece of paper and a pencil and write down all the good things about yourself. Don't be modest. Imagine that you're preparing an obituary and you're trying to pick up and expose all your own good points. When you've done that try and think of the worst faults that your enemies could find in your behaviour and make a list of those. Then compare the two lists. If you've been honest you'll probably be pleasantly surprised to see that the good points far outweigh the bad points. You may be a little obsessive, rather cautious and perhaps even difficult to get on with. But those disadvantages will be more than outweighed by your honesty, generosity and capacity for hard work.

Once you've recognized that you do have good points,

that you do have something to offer and that you need not automatically consider yourself inferior to all those around you, then you will be in a much stronger position to avoid being manoeuvred into the sort of positions where guilt is inescapable.

Express your guilt

Like many of the forces which influence our lives guilt does far more damage when kept secret. Within us it can only do harm, producing a wide variety of emotional responses. If, on the other hand, we do our best to express our guilt we will usually find that the damage can be minimized.

There are many different ways in which guilt can be expressed. We can confess our guilt to some suitable confessor. At various times and in various societies we have chosen many different confessors. Today some choose priests while others prefer psychotherapists; the end result is, however, much the same. By reporting our guilt and our suspected sin we can to a certain extent exorcize the ghost of that guilt, acquiring instead forgiveness and understanding.

However, whether it be manned by a cleric or a physician the confessional does not answer all our problems. If we confess to our priest that we have contemplated an abortion the priest will only offer absolution if he is convinced that we are truly repentant. The forgiveness on offer has strings of its own. If we make our confession to a doctor, whether he be a friendly general practitioner or a formidable specialist psychiatrist, we may well have to make do with the confession being an end in itself. Doctors who have little or no experience may be tempted to offer sympathy, understanding and encouragement, but on the whole the more experienced members of the medical profession can not easily be tempted into betraying any personal emotional response. Since, unlike the priest, they do not offer the tacit approval of any higher authority their value is strictly limited.

The most effective way to express our guilt is perhaps to share it with those whose love and respect we value. It is often said that a trouble shared is a trouble halved and it is not difficult to see the truth in that particular adage. The fact is that to discuss our guilt with others we must first accept the fact that there is some external cause; whether that cause be a personal relationship or a social force. And the best chance of finding support in our time of need is to then discuss our guilt with someone who understands exactly what we are talking about. No professional confessor working in neat and antiseptic isolation can offer the same mixture of encouragement, approval and sympathy as a good friend.

The guilt that is allowed to go unrecognized and unexposed will grow inside until it gets out of all proportion and begins to destroy us. Identifying the source of our guilt, sharing it, exposing it to the outside world and allowing it to be studied in some detail can in some instances prove remarkably therapeutic.

Often the very fact that the guilt has been recognized, rather than discussed or dissected, will be enough to stunt its growth. There is no guilt more destructive or dangerous than one that is allowed to remain hidden. And there is no destructive or dangerous guilt that cannot be tamed by being exposed. It is this need to expose guilt that provokes murderers and burglars to confess years after their crimes have been committed and long since filed away in some forgotten drawer.

Policemen and detectives of all kinds know very well that criminals will often be forced to confess their guilt to someone, even if their confession leads eventually to their own conviction. The fact is that the pain of keeping the guilt a hidden secret is so great that any alternative is preferable. What is true for criminals and their specific guilts is also true for those of us whose guilts are less conventional and more difficult to punish or forgive.

Given time unexposed guilts can undoubtedly grow to quite a remarkable extent. For example, I remember once seeing a man whose life had been consumed by his own particular secret guilt. As a young soldier he had spent many years parted from his bride and while serving abroad he had several times spent nights with whores. As a result of one such adventure he had contracted a venereal disease and needed treatment with penicillin.

He stored the memory away on his return and told no one, least of all his wife. When their son was born deaf and dumb he was convinced that the damage had been done by the infection he'd caught. Slowly over the years the guilt grew alongside his son and when I saw that unhappy man his life was almost unbearable.

In fact, if he had been able to share his fears and his guilt when they'd first begun to bite he would have saved himself incalculable pain. The boy's deformity had nothing to do with his venereal infection. Anyone with a modicum of medical training could have told him that.

I remember another patient too who nursed a secret for too many years. As a young man he'd driven home half drunk from a late night party and had read in the following morning's paper of an old lady who'd been knocked down and killed on the route he'd followed.

His feeling of guilt had been intensified by finding a dent in one front wing of his car. His fear of the consequences had, however, been greater than his fear of his own conscience and he'd kept his secret for twenty years. Eventually it proved too much for him and he killed himself leaving a note explaining why, next to the empty aspirin bottle.

It took the police no more than twenty minutes to prove that the old lady couldn't have been killed by his car. The newspaper report had been inaccurate. She'd died the night before my patient had acquired his dent.

Don't put too many demands on yourself

I doubt if at any other time in history people have ever been made more aware of their responsibilities than they are today. As the months and years go by it seems that the number of people telling us what to do and what to think increases without any sort of restraint. So now in addition to our basic responsibilities to our parents, our children, our lovers, and our friends, we also have an unending series of responsibilities to all those around us. And as if that were not enough we also have to listen to the arguments, pleas and demands of the unending series of experts who are only too willing to give us the benefit of their wisdom and experience.

As parents we learn that we should teach our children to read as soon as they can walk; that to teach them too much puts too great a strain on their young minds; that we should give them vitamin supplements; we are told that we shouldn't expose their bodies to too many drugs; we are warned of the dangers of adding fluoride to the water and of the dangers of not adding fluoride to the water; we are encouraged to force them to exercise and to let them do their own thing; to allow them freedom of choice and to ensure that they read the right sort of books and don't watch too much television.

As children we are taught of our many and varied responsibilities to our parents; as consumers we are taught of our responsibilities to manufacturers, retailers and other consumers; as wives or husbands we are taught of our responsibilities to our spouses and as voters we are constantly reminded of our responsibilities to the State.

The demands are so varied, so numerous and so conflicting that it is quite impossible for any one individual to obey them all. How, for example, can a young married woman with two small children be expected to obey all the responsibilities she is told that she has? If she goes out to

72

work and fulfils her obligations to other members of her sex she will be failing in her responsibilities to her family. If she stays at home and looks after her husband and her children she will surely be failing her sisters.

All these pressures, all these forces, produce guilt of their own. And in the end those who fail to satisfy all these demands will begin to feel guilty for having failed. That is the ultimate guilt, the most unavoidable and most destructive guilt of them all.

The only way to avoid it is to choose priorities and to refuse to be steamrolled into accepting too many demands or too many responsibilities. There is no one individual alive who could cope with all the expectations of our modern society. We must all make decisions and choose priorities. And once the priorities have been selected then we have to be prepared to operate them. For example, the man who has a demanding job and a family must make some decision about what comes first. There will be times when the demands of the job will come into conflict with the demands of his family. He has to know which will come first. If he tries to satisfy both the chances are that he will fail both.

Learning to balance these varied demands is a vital part of learning to deal with guilt. When recognized and controlled and accepted in limited quantities guilt can be a useful and powerful force. When allowed to accumulate endlessly guilts can prove too much even for the strongest individual.

George Turpin, for example, was a wealthy businessman with many remarkable talents. But he could never learn to limit his own responsibilities and he seemed quite incapable of ever controlling the amount of guilt he was prepared to accept. By the time I knew him he was racing around struggling to balance an unbelievable variety of different guilts. He was rather like one of those men in circuses who run around balancing spinning plates on sticks.

73

He felt it his duty not only to look after his own family and his employees but also to take a personal interest in the welfare of just about everyone living in his community. He served on numerous committees and gave them all his attention. He worried endlessly about other people and spent hour after hour looking for ways to solve other people's problems. He never found time to relax or enjoy his life and seemed to carry the worries of the world on his shoulders.

If Mr Turpin had learned to limit the demands he put on himself and had been prepared to accept the fact that he could only accept a finite amount of responsibility he would have been able to do a great deal for a great many people. But he couldn't do that. He had been brought up in a family where money had never been scarce and he felt enormously guilty when he saw people living in poverty or in pain. It sometimes seemed to me that he blamed himself for everyone else's misfortunes.

In an impossible attempt to make up for the fact that his parents had accumulated almost untold wealth at the expense of their workforce Mr Turpin pushed himself beyond his own limitations; he died in his forties of a perforated duodenal ulcer. Ironically if he'd made fewer demands on himself more people would have benefited.

Get things into proportion

From time to time we all feel guilty about the most remarkable things and suffer the most enormous agonies as a result of what are in effect quite trivial deeds. I remember, for example, having an otherwise sane and sensible patient come to me suffering from quite severe depression as a result of the guilt she felt for having failed to make a fancy dress outfit for her young son.

He had been invited to go to a Christmas party dressed as a Roman soldier. Unfortunately, the fortnight before the

74

party was unbelievably hectic. My patient's mother was taken ill and rushed into hospital with gall bladder trouble. Her husband had to fly off to Spain at very short notice in order to cope with a crisis which had sprung up over some imported materials. She herself developed a quite bad chest infection and spent four days lying in bed unable to do anything at all.

As a result of all that activity she found herself on the night of the fancy dress party with no costume. She hurriedly dressed her young son in a piece of curtain material, a pair of her old sandals and a few laurel leaves picked from a garden bush. And then for weeks suffered an extraordinary and quite unreasonable amount of guilt because she thought she had failed to do her best for him. Despite his assurances and the fact that he had a splendid time at the party she allowed the incident to prey on her mind. It became a sort of symbol of her failure as a mother.

I don't think that the extent to which she had allowed the incident to get out of all proportion truly came home to her until one day when she asked her son if he had forgiven her for not producing a more effective costume and found that he had forgotten the party altogether.

Getting our guilts into proportion and seeing them in something approaching true perspective isn't always easy. There are, however, several little tricks that are worth trying if you have a tendency to allow things to get out of hand.

To begin with it is sometimes a good idea to try and imagine just how you would feel if someone else was guilty of the sort of crime for which you are blaming yourself. For example, I remember very well seeing a woman in her early thirties who was suffering enormously because she had failed to invite all her husband's relatives to stay for Christmas Day. He had a large family and each year since their marriage they had all arrived, stayed for eight or ten hours and disappeared almost without a word of thanks.

Eventually it got too much and Mrs Garrard, my patient, put her foot down firmly. No more relatives, she insisted. Her husband didn't mind and neither did anyone else in her immediate family.

By the middle of January, however, Mrs Garrard was consumed by guilt. She didn't just feel that her husband's relatives had been upset by the change but she also felt sure that anyone else who heard about what she'd done would be bound to think her unreasonable, rude and uncharitable.

'What would you say' I asked her, 'if I told you that a neighbour of mine did exactly the same thing last Christmas?'

'It's nothing to do with me,' shrugged Mrs Garrard. 'I don't see why I should say anything.'

'And what would you say,' I went on, 'if I told you that I didn't invite my wife's relatives this year?'

'I wouldn't blame you at all if they're anything like my husband's folks,' she smiled.

'And what if you knew that your next-door-neighbour had had a blazing row with her mother-in-law?'

'I'd think that her mother-in-law probably got what she deserved,' she confessed.

'So if you don't feel contempt, hatred or anything else exceptionally strong for my neighbour, me and your neighbour, why should any of us despise you for what you did?' I asked her.

'I see what you mean,' she nodded. A relatively minor social incident had suddenly been seen for what it was worth.

Putting things into perspective in this way can be most valuable for the simple but important reason that we often do find it difficult to see things as they really are. You may feel that you've let the children down if you don't buy them vitamin-enriched cornflakes, if you don't take them to school in a freshly polished car or if you don't buy them

76

sweets every day, but would you think any the less of anyone else for failing to do any of these things?

The truth is that we often torture ourselves quite un-
necessarily.

One day to live

Another trick, useful for putting things in perspective, is to
look at your guilt and try to imagine just how important it
would be if you had just one day left to live.

If you feel guilty because you haven't visited your Uncle
Sidney, because you haven't bought the neighbours an
Easter card, because you haven't cleaned out your office
drawer, because you haven't emptied the sweet papers out
of the glove compartment in the car or because you haven't
tidied the tool shed do you still think that any one of those
things would matter if you had just one day left to live?

Seen in that sort of perspective don't these guilts look
slightly silly? Similarly, if you had just one day left to live
would you honestly spend much time worrying about
whether or not your vote in one of the most recent national
or local elections was a damaging error or about whether or
not buying a foreign car has put thousands of jobs in
jeopardy?

These are the sort of things many people do feel guilty
about. But are they problems that are really worth worrying about? And is your suffering going to make any difference? I think that most of us, if we had just one day left to
live would spend our hours on other more enjoyable activities.

Alternatively take a look at your guilt and try to see just
how important it would be if you knew that you had
another thousand years to live. Put into that sort of time
scale most of the things that most of us spend most of our
time thinking about look remarkably trivial. After all, is it
really going to make all that much difference to the history

77

of the world if the laundry is picked up today or tomorrow? Is it truly likely to change anything very much if the apple trees aren't pruned until next week? Is it likely to damage the next generation if the garden weeds are given another week's grace? Or is an orgasm here or there likely to be remembered as a major event in your life? Is a forgotten birthday card all that significant in those sort of terms?

Actually you don't even need to put things into a thousand year history to see them in some sort of perspective. You can get very much the same sort of effect by trying to imagine just how significant things will look in a mere five years time.

You'll quickly see that very many of the things you feel guilty about are really of remarkably little importance. And you'll also be able to see which things are of importance and do need to be taken seriously. You may also be surprised to realize just how much valuable thinking time you waste on trivial problems and just how little attention you give to important decisions which may really affect your future and the future of those around you.

Only human

Guilt can be extremely damaging. It can produce an enormous range of mental and physical disabilities. It can produce pain and shame and have a tremendous effect on our lives. But despite all that it is important to remember that guilt is an essentially human emotion. And the more civilized a community and the more civilized the man the greater the guilt he is likely to bear. Guilt is an essential companion to love and friendship and it is the emotional response which is in turn the creative force behind many of our most valuable human attributes.

If it were not for the existence of guilt human society could not exist as we know it today. Individuals who do not experience guilt know nothing of shame and fear, anxiety

78

or affection. They behave selfishly and dishonestly without guilt to restrict their activities. They can run roughshod over all around them without any personal restraint because they have no sense of right or wrong. They are incapable of respect or admiration, righteous anger or true courage. A society of people who know no guilt would be unacceptably cruel and unreasonably harsh and would not, indeed, be described as a true society.

We should not, therefore, be ashamed of our guilt nor seek to avoid it altogether. But we should, I believe, learn to try and control it and to limit the damage it can do. Uncontrolled guilt can be damaging, dispiriting and destructive. But when controlled, guilt can prove to be a powerful and effective driving force. Some of the greatest men and women who have ever lived have been consumed by guilt. For many, part of their greatness has come from their ability to control and use their guilt as a positive rather than a negative force.

As we have seen when guilt is allowed to run riot it can harm both the mind and the body. It can, however, also be harnessed and used to great effect. For it is an undoubted fact that the fear of failure which so often results from guilt, the insecurity that is a common companion to guilt, and the inferiority which is also a common consequence are all powerful forces which can produce success and great achievements of all kinds. Those who know guilt and who are aware of its power as a formative influence are in some ways lucky for they are blessed with a power which will enable them to cope with crises, deal with problems and rise above uncertainties that would prove to be impossible obstacles to men and women without such a powerful internal driving force.

To harness our guilt we must learn to acknowledge the various sources, to discipline ourselves to differentiate between the relevant and the irrelevant, to strengthen our capacity to cope with guilt by building up our own defences, to choose which demands we are prepared to accept and to put our guilt into proportion and perspective.

Guilt can often cause great pain. It can, however, be an irresistible power and an enviable force.

7

A Counter-Guilt Philosophy

Here is a simple ten-step programme of advice for all guilt-sufferers which can be applied to any guilt problem.

Step One: Ask yourself if you feel guilty because you have actually done something wrong or because you feel that in some nebulous way you have let down those close to you or those who expect you to behave in a certain way. This is a very important and fundamental question.

Step Two: When you have done something obviously wrong (however minor the deed may be) then there will usually be some explanation. You may have smashed into someone's parked car because you were hurrying to avoid being late for an important appointment. Or you may have dropped and broken a favourite piece of china because your hands were slippery. These are concrete errors and the solution can be as simple and obvious as your mistakes.

Once you have acknowledged the responsibility for your misdeed and accepted whatever penalties may be involved you should try and learn what you can from the event. If you've had a motoring accident rushing to an appointment then you can try and set out earlier next time. By learning from the event you reduce the chances of anything similar happening a second time. You should not allow yourself to feel guilty about whatever it is you've done. Guilt won't help you and it won't help anyone else. Indeed by feeling bad and losing your ability to concentrate you are likely to increase the likelihood of a second mishap. And don't feel guilty about not feeling guilty either!

If you have done something that you know is wrong you should apologize, pay whatever consequences there are and learn what you can from the incident. And that is all.

Recriminations do no one any good as we have seen.

Step Three: When you haven't committed any crime but are guilty in your own eyes only of a sin of omission then the chances are that you feel that way because someone else has *made* you feel that way. There is no wrong doing that you can define. Nothing for which you can make reparation. And no opportunity for you to learn from the experience.

This is the type of guilt which causes most pain. And it is the type of guilt which is most difficult to get rid of. There are many sources of such guilt, but the one thing that the guilt always carries with it is a feeling that someone else has suffered because of something you've done or not done. Often it is something that you've not done.

To deal effectively with this type of guilt you must find and isolate the cause. After all if you felt bad because you'd broken something and you didn't know what it was you'd find it difficult to do anything about it. Once you've isolated the cause of your guilt and identified that cause as a parent, a friend or a religion then you can begin to deal with your guilt more effectively.

Step Four: Learn to differentiate between the realistic expectations of those close to you and the purely selfish desires they may harbour. You should learn to identify the people who are most likely to make unreasonable demands. And you should make it clear to them that you are not prepared to put your conscience at their disposal.

Similarly you should not be afraid to make it clear to those who may want to put you under pressure that you are not prepared to feel guilty every time you fail to satisfy the aspirations and expectations of the groups or societies they claim to represent. Define your own ambitions and moral standards and you'll limit the extent to which your conscience is committed.

Step Five: Whatever you have done wrong you should remember that you are only human and that human beings have a tendency to make mistakes. You don't have to vilify yourself because you've broken a vase or go into deep personal mourning because you've failed to keep up with the Joneses. Don't put too many demands on yourself and don't let others put too many demands on you either.

When you recognize that you have done something wrong you should do all you can to ensure that you learn from the experience and that you minimize the chance of there being a second error of the same kind. That's all that you, or anyone else, can expect.

Step Six: Don't punish yourself unreasonably. Try to imagine yourself as an observer. How would you feel if someone else had done what you've done? Would you forgive? Would you really be as hard on them as you are being on yourself?

It is sometimes said that charity should begin at home. I think that perhaps we should say that compassion should also begin at home. Try to be fair to yourself.

Step Seven: If people close to you keep making you feel guilty make it clear to them that you're not prepared to stand for it. Don't keep making excuses for people who consistently make you feel guilty. No one has a right to make other people suffer. And however well disposed you may feel towards them I'm afraid that the individual who is always filling you with guilt is either stupid, greedy, selfish or wicked.

A friend who is always making you feel guilty is no friend at all.

Step Eight: In ten years will your guilt still be justified? Will your evil deed still look that black? The ten year test is really a very useful way to put things into perspective. Just try to imagine how significant your wrong doing will appear in the future and just how much a part it will have played in your life and in the lives of those around you. You'll probably be surprised to realize that put in context it really isn't as significant as you thought it was.

Step Nine: You have rights as an individual and you shouldn't forget that those rights exist. Whether you are a mother, a father, a child, an employee, an employer, a schoolteacher, a doctor, or a chauffeur you are also YOU. You have a right to enjoy your life and to expect those around you to respect your rights. You have a right to expect other people to treat you as you treat them. You have a right to expect others not to make unreasonable demands on you. You have a right to make some decisions without thinking of everyone around you.

Dealing effectively with guilt means getting the right balance between your conscience, your responsibilities, your love for those close to you, your willingness to please at any cost, your desire not to see others get hurt, and your own rights as an individual. That doesn't mean that you should never do things you don't want to do. But simply that you should remember that you have rights too. And if you're the sort of person who suffers a lot from guilt then you're probably also the sort of person who doesn't pay too much attention to your own individual rights.

Step Ten: Don't underrate yourself. The type of people who suffer most from guilt really do have a lot going for them. They tend to be honest, hard working, generous and gentle. So spend a little time looking at your own good points instead of concentrating on your faults!

The chances are that you have a good deal more going for you than you've ever realized. Learn to treat yourself to a touch of pride every now and again!

Index

Heart disease 8, 59
Homosexuals 25–6

Impotence 24
Inadequacy, feelings of 1, 8, 25
Inferiority 51, 52–5, 65, 79
Influence
  maternal 15
  in relationships 65
  Roman Catholic Church 33
  school teachers 36–7
Insecurity 51, 55, 65, 79
Internal phenomenon 2, 3

Jealousy 65

Lesbian 25
Love 1, 4, 5, 64, 78
Loyalties, divided 20–2

Memories 31
Men
  attitudes to women 12
  repressive behaviour 40
  sexual problems 24–5
Mental stress 8, 60
Mental traumas 56, 57
Mothers, working 18–20

Nervous breakdown 7–8, 11
Nudity 39, 40

Obsession 1
Operations, life saving 42–3
Orgasm 24, 78

Parents
  debt to 16
  expectations of 49
  relationship with children
    14–20, 62–3
  responsibilities 72–4
Penance 3
Perspective, true 75–8, 80, 83–4
Physical disorders 8, 10, 57
Physical illnesses 57, 59, 60

Prejudices 12, 13, 36, 37
Pressures
  commercial 45–8, 65
  modern 41–4
  parental 16
  social 50
Pride 84
Priests 2, 3, 12, 32, 69
Priorities 73
Promotion 7
Prostitutes 40
Psychopaths 1, 10
Psychotherapists 69
Punishment 17

Redundancy 44
Regret 1
Relationships
  business 28–30
  friends 26–8, 63–5, 83
  homosexual 25–6
  new 8–9
  parents and children 14–20,
    62–6
  personal 11, 13, 49, 65, 70
  sexual 9, 22
  social 27
Relatives 27, 42, 64, 75–6
Religion 12, 65, 82
Religious teachings 32–5, 41
Resentment 19, 21
Responsibilities 20, 72–4, 84
Restraint, personal 60, 79
Rights, individual 84
Roman Catholic Church 33

School teachers 12, 35–7
Self-assurance 67, 68
Self-confidence 12, 68
Self-consciousness 68
Self-criticism 1, 2
Self-pity 56
Self-recrimination 2
Sex 22–6, 38, 40

Overcoming Common Problems Series

Overcoming Common Problems Series

Overcoming Common Problems Series

The Parkinson's Disease Handbook
DR RICHARD GODWIN-AUSTEN

Second Wife, Second Best?
Managing your marriage as a second wife
GLYNNIS WALKER

Self-Help for your Arthritis
EDNA PEMBLE

Six Weeks to a Healthy Back
ALEXANDER MELLEBY

Sleep Like a Dream – The Drug-free Way
ROSEMARY NICOL

Solving your Personal Problems
PETER HONEY

Someone to Love
How to find romance in the personal columns
MARGARET NELSON

A Step-Parent's Handbook
KATE RAPHAEL

Stress and your Stomach
DR VERNON COLEMAN

Trying to Have a Baby?
Overcoming infertility and child loss
MAGGIE JONES

What Everyone Should Know about Drugs
KENNETH LEECH

Why Be Afraid?
How to overcome your fears
DR PAUL HAUCK

You and Your Varicose Veins
DR PATRICIA GILBERT

Your Arthritic Hip and You
GEORGE TARGET